3

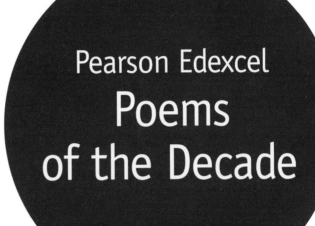

Pearson Edexcel
Poems of the Decade

Richard Vardy

Series Editors:
Nicola Onyett and Luke McBratney

HODDER
EDUCATION
AN HACHETTE UK COMPANY

Hachette UK's policy is to use papers that are natural, renewable and recyclable products and made from wood grown in well-managed forests and other controlled sources. The logging and manufacturing processes are expected to conform to the environmental regulations of the country of origin.

Orders: please contact Bookpoint Ltd, 130 Park Drive, Milton Park, Abingdon, Oxon OX14 4SE. Telephone: +44 (0)1235 827827. Fax: +44 (0)1235 400401. Email education@bookpoint.co.uk Lines are open from 9 a.m. to 5 p.m., Monday to Saturday, with a 24-hour message answering service. You can also order through our website: www.hoddereducation.co.uk

ISBN: 978 1 5104 5269 5

© Richard Vardy 2019

First published in 2019 by

Hodder Education

An Hachette UK Company,

Carmelite House, 50 Victoria Embankment

London EC4Y 0LS

Impression number	5	4	3	2	1
Year	2023	2022	2021	2020	2019

Cover photo ©HIROSHI H - stock.adobe.com

Typeset by Integra Software Services Pvt. Ltd., Pondicherry, India

Printed by Bell & Bain Ltd, Glasgow

A catalogue record for this title is available from the British Library.

Contents

Using this guide

Why read this guide?

The purposes of this A-level Literature Guide are to enable you to organise your thoughts and responses to the set poems from *Poems of the Decade: An Anthology of the Forward Books of Poetry 2002–2011*, a set text for Pearson Edexcel specification, to deepen your understanding and enjoyment of the poems and to help you to address the requirements of the exam in order to achieve the best possible grade.

You should note that teachers and examiners are most interested in reading an *informed personal response to the text*. A guide such as this can help you to understand the poems, form your own opinions and suggest further areas to think about, but it cannot replace your *own* ideas and responses as an informed reader.

How to make the most of this guide

You should adopt the above advice to your individual reading of the poems. The chapter entitled 'The poems and poem commentaries' helps you to consolidate and extend your own appreciation of the poems, as well as offer you a range of approaches to analysis and interpretation. After you have formulated an individual response to a poem, you might then like to read the relevant poem commentary.

The 'Comparing themes' and 'Comparing poets' methods' chapters are focused on making connections between the set poems from *Poems of the Decade*. This will help you particularly if you are studying the poems for AS-level. 'Responding to an unseen poem' will guide you through a suggested process of reading, interpreting, analysing and writing about an unseen poem under timed conditions. This will particularly help you if you are studying for the A-level exam. The final chapters will present you with a range of responses to the set poems with accompanying detailed commentaries.

It is vital that you familiarise yourself with the ways the exam board (Pearson Edexcel) assesses your essays on the poems. You should therefore use the specification and the sample assessment materials as your definitive guide to what you need to study and how you will be examined.

Studying *Poems of the Decade* for A-level

Bear in mind the sort of questions you are going to face in the examination. For the A-level exam, you will write one essay from a choice of two questions. Each question will ask you to compare an 'unseen' poem – a poem you are unlikely to have read – with one of the studied poems from *Poems of the Decade*. The question is likely to invite you to compare a common theme, idea, subject or method between the two poems. All poems that relate to the two questions will be printed in the examination paper. This means that, to be prepared for the exam you must know every single one of the studied poems, and be able to interpret, analyse and make connections with a poem you have not read before.

Studying *Poems of the Decade* for AS-level

If you are taking the AS qualification, the questions on *Poems of the Decade* will invite you to compare a common theme, idea, subject or method between any two of the poems you have studied. One poem will be specified, but you will need to choose the second yourself. The poems will not be printed in the examination – you will need to bring in a clean, unannotated copy of the studied poems. You will choose to answer one question from a choice of two. This means that, to be prepared for the exam, you must know every single one of the studied poems. Since the question will ask you to choose a second poem, you should also prepare by making a range of connections between the different poems and grouping them into different categories.

Key elements

This guide is designed to help you to raise your achievement in your examination response to *Poems of the Decade: An Anthology of the Forward Books of Poetry 2002–2011*. It is intended for you to use throughout your AS or A-level English Literature course. It will help you when you are studying the poems for the first time, and also during your revision.

The following features have therefore been used throughout this guide, to help you focus and extend your understanding and appreciation of the poems:

Context

Context boxes give interesting contextual information that relates to particular aspects of the poem.

TASK

Tasks are short and focused. They allow you to engage directly with a particular aspect of the poem.

Build critical skills

Broaden your thinking about the poem by answering questions in the **Build critical skills** boxes. These help you to consider your own opinions in order to develop your skills of criticism and analysis.

Taking it further ▶

Taking it further boxes suggest and provide further background or illuminating parallels to the poem.

CRITICAL VIEW

Critical view boxes highlight a particular critical viewpoint that will help to shed new light on the poem. This allows you to develop the higher-level skills needed to come up with your own interpretation of the poem.

Introduction: reading poetry

What is a poem?

A poem is not a maths equation to be solved by you, a teacher or a critic. Nor is poetry written to be studied in a classroom or analysed in an exam. First and foremost, poetry is an art form to be read for *pleasure and enjoyment*, in the same way we might enjoy a piece of music or take pleasure in looking at a painting.

A painter's raw material is colour; a poet's raw material is language. Poetry can therefore be quite dense as the poet seeks to surprise, play – or even conceal – with language. Poetry is musical and rhythmical. It also looks visually different on the page, as poets use form and space as a key part of their craft.

It is no surprise then that a poem rewards repeated, careful readings – different ideas and patterns often delightfully reveal themselves with each reading. This is a fundamental part of the pleasure of reading poetry.

Although poems are all located in a tradition which stretches back thousands of years, it is worth bearing in mind the poems in the anthology were all written in the 21st century. Compared to the poetry of, say, William Wordsworth or Christina Rossetti, the range of references are, perhaps, much closer to your own experiences: Post-it notes, full-fat milk, barbecue fluid, call-centres, dodgems. The anthology reminds us that our everyday experiences, the ordinary and the modern, are worthy – and enjoyable – subjects for poetry.

The first reading

Start by just looking at the poem. A quick glance at Patience Agbabi's 'Eat Me' will reveal a tight, regular form; a quick glance at John Burnside's 'History' will reveal the opposite! The shape of a poem may (or may not) suggest something about the poem or its idea; in the case of 'History', the irregularity and gaps on the page may imply impermanence or fragmentation – key ideas in the poem itself.

It is also worth considering the title before you begin reading – again, it might provide an interesting 'way in' to the poem. What might the title of 'From the Journal of a Disappointed Man' indicate about the poem itself? How does it contrast with, say, 'Look We Have Coming to Dover!'?

You should now be in a position to read the poem for the first time. Read it out loud wherever possible. In a classroom, try reading it to your partner or in a group, or hearing your teacher read it. If possible, listen to a recording by the poet or an actor. Remember, poetry has a musical quality – its ancient roots are in the oral tradition of songs and story-telling, therefore sound (and silence) has always been an essential part of a poem's impact.

Taking it further ▶

The Poetry Archive (**www.poetryarchive.com**) is a wonderful website containing thousands of recordings of contemporary poets reading their own work, including many of the poets in the anthology. Hearing a poet read can shed new and interesting light on the poem itself.

After your preliminary reading, it is a good idea to jot down some initial notes about the poem's overall tone and maybe its 'meaning', but avoid jumping to conclusions. Equally, do not feel compelled to 'get it' the first time round. Tolerate misunderstanding, unusual words and uncertainty. Uncertainty – or ambiguity – is prevalent in many poems in the collection. Part of the joy of, say, 'The Lammas Hireling' is that we can never be 100 per cent certain about what the speaker did to the hireling, or even whether we should believe his story at all.

Re-reading and re-reading

Build on your preliminary ideas by frequent re-reading. Part of the pleasure of reading a poem lies in noticing new aspects each time you revisit it.

Try to become a slow reader. Follow the sense of the poem; when a line is enjambed – that is, it does not end with a punctuation mark – carry on without stopping to the next line. Be guided by punctuation – if there is a full stop, pause and consider what the sentence has expressed. Lines of poetry, and indeed stanzas, are not usually intended as stand-alone units of sense. If you lose the overall sense at any point, go back to the beginning of the sentence and read again from there. Be patient – slow reading gets you further than lots of skim reads.

With each reading, be prepared to change your mind and continue to be open-minded. Note down any question or queries which might arise. You could ask other students in your class or your teacher these questions, and you could conduct further research of your own.

The big picture

After a number of readings, you may be able to outline tentatively the situation presented in the poem. Many of the poems in the *Poems of the Decade* selection have at their core experiences, memories and objects.

You might then be in a position to identify the key concerns and themes of the poem. Poetry, like all art forms, tends to explore key aspects of the human condition, such as love, death or memory. Many poems adopt a particular attitude (or attitudes) towards these themes. For example, through exploring the object of a handkerchief, the poem 'Material' is reflecting on motherhood, specifically the distances across time between generations and the different ways of parenting.

This is the skill of interpretation – of working out key implications and ideas in the poem. It will help for you to have this overall sense of the poem before you explore its details.

The detail and the effects

As you continue to re-read, consider the methods the poet uses to shape meanings and create effects. In the exam, you will be expected to explore the techniques used; however, you should definitely avoid using any kind of checklist of features to seek in every poem. Instead, allow the poem to suggest which features to explore: 'Chainsaw Versus the Pampas Grass' makes extensive use of figurative imagery, whereas 'Giuseppe' barely uses any. Consider features which are of most importance to the poem's overall meaning and ideas.

An interesting question to ask is: who is the 'speaker' of the poem? In some personal lyric poems, such as 'Effects', we can assume the speaker is aligned closely to the poet. However, in poems such as 'Eat Me' and 'The Lammas Hireling', the speaker is a dynamic, constructed character, and we should perhaps assume some kind of critical distance between the speaker and the poet. Perhaps you can also work out who the speaker is talking to (known as the addressee). Identifying the speaker may also lead to reflections on the tone of the poem: is it angry and frustrated, like in 'Please Hold'? Or is it detached and critical, like in 'Journal of a Disappointed Man'? Or maybe the tone changes or is inconsistent, like the movement between humour and seriousness in 'Ode on a Grayson Perry Urn'.

You may already have noted the shape of the poem in your earlier reading, but now that you are more familiar with the text, this can perhaps repay further reflection. The shape of the poem is also called the poem's form. Consider the line lengths and number of lines per stanza. You should also consider whether or not the poem has a regular or irregular form. Purposefully analysing form – considering how it adds to the meaning and impact of the poem – can be difficult, so beware of falling into the trap of feature spotting.

Often, considering the diction – word choices – can be very fruitful. Note, for example, the significance of Tishani Doshi's choice of verbs, especially the one used in the final line of 'The Deliverer'. You should also be sensitive to any repetition of words, or other patterns across the poem.

Consider imagery. How has the poet used figurative language, personification, symbolism or descriptive language which summons pictures (or sounds and smells) as we read? Bearing in mind the inherent musical quality of poetry, you should give some thought to the poem's use of sound, such as rhythm, rhyme, pauses and alliteration.

Making connections

Both the AS and the A-level specifications require you to make connections between poems. Poets may well explore similar subject matter – such as memorable experiences, or the death of a loved one – but go about it in very different ways. Compare not just the attitudes towards the shared subject, but the methods used. For example, one poem may use a lot of figurative devices, whereas another could be simpler and more direct in its phrasing. The comparative process nearly always provides new insights into both poems, where you notice things you would otherwise have missed.

The poems and poem commentaries

Target your thinking

As you read each summary and commentary, ask yourself the following questions:

- What is your considered personal response to the poem – what do you think are its main concerns? (**AO1**)
- How can you use literary terminology to help you to articulate your responses with more precision and concision? (**AO1**)
- Consider the most important methods that the poet uses in the poem: how does the poet use them to shape meaning and create effects? (**AO2**)
- In what ways can you connect the poem's themes, idea or methods to other poems in *Poems of the Decade*, or to your wider reading of 21st-century poetry? (**AO4**)

Patience Agbabi, 'Eat Me'

The **speaker** recounts the ways in which a man, presumably her partner, insists she eats a lot of food because he likes 'big girls'. At the beginning of the poem, the speaker weighs 30 stone. She is so large that she cannot leave the house. The day she becomes 39 stone, after having olive oil poured down her throat, the speaker rolls over on top of her partner – presumably during sex. Her weight suffocates him and he dies. Six hours later, the speaker is left contemplating eating his dead body.

Commentary With its echoes of a grisly fairy tale, this gleefully macabre poem is an exploration of power – specifically the sexual power dynamics between men and women. The speaker is initially presented as passive. She does as she is told uncomplainingly. Indeed, her only pleasure is reduced to the 'rush of fast food'. The female speaker is objectified by the gaze of her male partner, as he asks her to walk around the bed so that he can watch her 'broad / belly wobble'. However, the dynamic starts to shift in the eighth **tercet** as the speaker 'allowed him to stroke / my globe of a cheek'. The speaker now has the power as she appears to use her partner's desire and 'greed' against him. This is given ultimate expression in his suffocation during sex and her probable cannibalism of him.

The poem makes use of a **persona**: the speaker is a distinctive character in her own right. Alongside the direct speech of the partner ('Open wide') there is a strong sense of a spoken voice throughout: **colloquialisms** ('When I hit thirty'); elliptical sentences ('Didn't even taste it'); frequent simple, direct sentences ('I was his Jacuzzi') which seem to suggest the speaker's uncritical, unreflective acceptance of the situation.

Context

The situation described in the poem is by no means unique. There is a recognised condition (sometimes referred to as 'Feederism') in which a person (usually but not always a male) is sexually aroused by their partner gaining excessive body fat.

Juggernaut: a large, heavy vehicle – usually a lorry; interestingly, it also has a wider meaning of a powerful, destructive force.

Breadfruit: a tropical fruit, typically found in the islands of the Caribbean or the Pacific.

Despite its skill in capturing the voice of the narrator, the poem is tightly structured and has a very regular **form**. It is written in tercets with **assonantal half-rhyme** (for example, the short 'e' sound in 'shipwreck … bed … flesh') and a regular scheme (AAA). The tercets each end with a full stop, with the notable exception of the sixth, where the **enjambment** perhaps represents the 'tidal wave of flesh' spreading out. The exuberance of the language – and the excesses described in the narrative itself – are therefore in a dynamic tension with this highly controlled and regular form.

Agbabi also deploys a remarkable array of sound effects. For example, the **alliteration** in 'judder like a juggernaut' seems to make the line itself wobble. Note also the sensuous **fricatives** and repetition in 'His flesh, my flesh flowed' to describe their sex together. Agbabi also uses simple repetition to chilling effect as the male partner says: 'I like / big girls, soft girls, girls I can burrow inside'. There is also **anaphora** in the seventh stanza: 'too fat to leave … too fat to use fat … too fat to be called chubby', which reinforces the excesses of her consumption as well as her powerlessness. The final stanza consists of three consecutive **end-stopped lines**. The pace therefore slows as the poem leads towards its final, shocking line, which acts almost as a gruesome punch-line to the absurd situation described: 'There was nothing else left in the house to eat.' The end-stopped lines might also indicate the speaker's growing confidence and power.

The speaker describes herself as swelling 'like forbidden fruit': the **allusion** to the Garden of Eden in this **simile** links their relationship to a particularly illicit desire, and perhaps foreshadows the disastrous consequences. Perhaps surprisingly, there is also a recurring pattern of **figurative images** associated with the sea and the exotic. Note the remarkable sequence of **metaphors** in the sixth stanza: 'His breadfruit', 'His desert island', 'a beached whale', 'a tidal wave'. Her body is her partner's possession, and the traditional natural poetic **images** of female objectification are – like much else in the poem – taken to extremes. The images also suggest both incapacity ('beached whale') and power ('tidal wave'). The partner's fattening up of the woman ultimately destroys him. This nautical **conceit** is extended in the metaphorical reference to 'my globe of a cheek' and in the image of drowning. Her suffocation of him is described as a silencing of his language, his authority and, therefore, his claims on her: she 'drowned his dying sentence out'.

CRITICAL VIEW

Some readers think the poem is less about gender politics and more an **allegory** of colonialism, where the male partner in the poem stands as a colonial authority (such as Britain in the 19th century) and the speaker is a colony. What evidence can you find to support this view? Do you find this interpretation convincing?

Simon Armitage, 'Chainsaw Versus the Pampas Grass'

The poem begins by describing in detail how a chainsaw is prepared – it is taken from its hook, oiled and attached to a power chord. The speaker turns on the chainsaw, which comes powerfully to life. The chainsaw destroys the pampas grass easily. The speaker then sets fire to what is left of the grass. Soon, however, the pampas grass grows back and the chainsaw remains on its hook below the stairs.

Commentary Typically for Armitage, this poem uses a persona because it adopts the vibrant voice of someone we can consider, in varying degrees, to be separate from Armitage himself. The speaker in the poem – drawn towards the power of the vividly described chainsaw – relishes the destruction of the pampas grass, but is made to look rather absurd as the pampas grass simply grows back. The pride and relish of the speaker is shown to be wildly – and humorously – misplaced.

In order to add a dynamic depth to this persona, the poem adopts a conversational tone. The sentence length varies dramatically – note the interesting **minor sentence** in the fifth stanza – 'Overkill', which seems to reinforce the speaker's pride. There are also frequent examples of colloquial idioms and expressions, such as 'finish things off', 'stealing the show' and 'I left it a year', which often serve to amplify the speaker's pride.

This impression of spoken voice is also reinforced by the irregular form. Armitage uses an apparently relaxed **free verse** as he varies line and stanza length markedly. The poem's form also confirms the excess and power that the poem describes, and so is matched closely to the content. Like the chainsaw itself, the stanzas – with their 'perfect disregard' for regularity and frequent enjambment – are straining to break free.

This is not to say that the poem is without carefully crafted patterns. The sentences shorten towards the end of the poem, as the speaker and chainsaw shrink back from their folly. Note also the anaphora in the third stanza – 'and felt', 'and felt' – emphasising the fear and awe the speaker feels for the chainsaw's power. There is also interesting syntactical patterning. To suggest the speaker's enthusiasm for the destruction, the clauses often begin with the subject 'I', followed by an -ed verb, especially in the fifth and sixth stanzas: 'I touched', 'I dabbed', 'I lifted', 'I ripped', 'I raked' and so on.

Perhaps the most distinctive feature of this poem, however, is its use of imagery. The **personification** of the chainsaw is clear: it is described as 'grinding its teeth'; it has a 'bloody desire' and a 'sweet tooth / for the flesh of the face'. A madman, perhaps, or a violent animal. In contrast, the pampas grass is personified as lordly, calm, self-contained: 'sunning itself' and 'wearing a new crown'.

'Chainsaw Versus the Pampas Grass' is clearly, therefore, a poem about power and conflict. The title alone confirms this. The violence of the chainsaw, the speaker's boastful pride, the pampas grass' quiet acquiescence and subsequent victory. However, we could also read the poem as an exploration of gender, of masculinity

Corn of Egypt: a saying to suggest that there is a lot of something. It has its origins in the Bible (Genesis 42.2).

▲ Pampas grass, 'with its ludicrous feathers / and plumes'. What would you say are the distinctive qualities of pampas grass? Why do you think Armitage decided to use this type of garden plant in his poem?

and femininity. We can ascribe traditional male behaviour to the actions of the speaker and the chainsaw. As though it were drinking a pint of lager, the chainsaw metaphorically 'knocked back a quarter-pint of engine oil'. Even its dreams are 'man-made'. The speaker is also stereotypically masculine in his exaggerated relish at severing and tearing the grass in a metaphorical and destructive 'game'. The feminine natural grass, meanwhile, has 'feathers / and plumes' (labelled, interestingly, as 'ludicrous' by the speaker) and is described dismissively as having 'footstools, cushions and tufts'. The grass is also described in very feminine terms as having a 'dark, secret / warmth' and is able to resist by closing and mending behind the blade, 'like cutting at water or air with a knife'. The pampas grass, of course, ultimately wins the battle and the speaker is described in the absurd, awkward position of looking on 'from the upstairs window like the midday moon' – suggesting how tentative and out-of-place he has become. What might this suggest about the version of masculinity as presented in the poem?

CRITICAL VIEW

The events could be read as a broader ecological comment on mankind's persistent and reckless attempts to maintain dominion over nature. Do you find this interpretation convincing? Is there any evidence to support this view?

Taking it further ▶

'Chainsaw Versus the Pampas Grass' shares many characteristics of mock-heroic poetry, in which deliberately mundane events are described in the elevated style of classical epic poetry. The effects are nearly always humorous and satirical. Perhaps the most famous example is 'The Rape of the Lock' written by Alexander Pope (1688–1744), which concerns the theft of a lock of hair from a young lady. Pope describes the incident as though it is comparable to an epic war. Look, for example, at the way Pope is describing the scissors below, used to cut the lock of hair:

> But when to mischief mortals bend their will,
>
> How soon they find fit instruments of ill!
>
> Just then, Clarissa drew with tempting grace
>
> A two-edg'd weapon from her shining case;
>
> So Ladies in Romance assist their Knight,
>
> Present the spear, and arm him for the fight.
>
> He takes the gift with rev'rence, and extends
>
> The little engine on his fingers' ends...

Conduct further research into the poem – and mock-heroic poetry in general. Why do you think Armitage chose to adopt this poetic genre for 'Chainsaw Versus the Pampas Grass'? How does it suit the subject of the poem?

Ros Barber, 'Material'

'Material' begins with a reflection on the cloth handkerchiefs used by the poet's mother. Barber associates these handkerchiefs initially with her own childhood, before changing the focus to a wider consideration of a vanished way of life associated with her mother's generation. The poet then contrasts the way she brings up her own children with the way her mother raised her. The poem concludes with Barber acknowledging that the modern way of living and parenting is her own 'material' to work with as best she can.

Commentary Barber begins with the object of a handkerchief, and uses it to explore a range of different ideas and experiences. The poem's chief concerns are with a lost history and the changing ways in which mothers bring up their children.

Barber correlates the disappearance of the handkerchief with a vanished world of department stores and headscarves. All are lost because 'those who used to buy them died'. Barber especially evokes this disappeared world in the concise character sketches in the fifth **octave**. These suggest a familiar, close-knit and supportive community of friends, family and neighbours. On the surface, Barber is mourning this lost way of life, with its 'soft and hidden history'. However, she avoids falling into the clichéd trap of arguing simply that everything was better in the past. Indeed, she even acknowledges that 'Nostalgia only makes me old'. Note the figurative and frightening 'painted talons' of Mrs White, or the rather deadened uniformity in her repeated instruction 'step-together, step-together, step-together'. Barber also remembers thinking handkerchiefs were the 'naffest Christmas gift you'd get' and an 'embarrassment of lace'.

The handkerchief is also closely associated with the poet's mother. The clear and direct opening line immediately establishes this as she is figuratively described as 'the hanky queen'. Barber presents her as loving and attentive; she would have a handkerchief, 'always, up her sleeve' to scrub against her face, or 'smudge the rouge'. Her gentle fondness for her mother is also reinforced in the humorous *image* of the hankies falling in love and mating, 'raising little squares'.

This contrasts with Barber's depiction of her own methods of parenting, represented by the 'scratchy and disposable' tissues bought from 'late-night garages and shops'. She lets her children watch television to give her time to work and she never wipes their noses. She even admits, in a self-critical rhetorical question in the eighth *octave*, to never having any tissues in her bag, let alone handkerchiefs. But there is more to it than a mere perceived shortcoming in her own character. The key line, reinforced by a rare instance of **caesura**, is at the beginning of the final *octave*: 'But it isn't mine. I'll let it go.' 'It', here, is the past, and her mother's way of bringing up her children. Barber recognises that the role of a mother has changed by the end of the 20th century: Barber works (pursuing a career as a lecturer and writer) and she must balance these demands with childcare. At the end of the poem, she imagines fondly her mother giving this advice: the paper tissues – modern motherhood, with all its pressures – are the only 'material' she has to work with.

TASK

Think about the different possible meanings of the title 'Material'. How does the title link with the ideas of the poem?

Build critical skills

How does Barber create a conversational tone to the poem? Find examples. What do you think are the effects of this tone?

Ros Barber has said that the poem 'Material' was originally intended to be a poem about the death of her mother, but she ended up writing a poem about handkerchiefs instead. This is perhaps because she wanted to avoid a painfully direct examination of her loss. Does this shed a new light on your reading of the poem? Do you think 'Material' could really be about Barber trying to come to terms with her mother's death?

'Material' is written in **octaves** with largely an ABCBDEFE rhyme (or half-rhyme) scheme (with the curious exception of the sixth stanza which has an extra line). Many lines are in **iambic tetrameter**, such as the opening three lines in the poem:

> My mother was the hanky queen
> when hanky meant a thing of cloth,
> not paper tissues bought in packs

Each stanza also ends with a full stop (again, with one exception) and is a statement of a separate, self-contained reflection or memory. A regular form such as this is associated with older, more traditional poetry, and so evokes the lost world being described, as well as recalling its restrictions.

Rhyming connects words together — there are rhymes in this poem which draw attention to a contrast, such as 'wool' and 'malls' or, perhaps, 'brood' and 'lassitude'. They might connect in other ways, such as 'purified' and 'died', or the particularly noteworthy final rhyme — 'disposable', 'material' and 'will' — three words which could be said to sum up the key ideas in the poem. Rhyme also underscores the often-humorous tone: 'not' and 'snot' being a particularly bathetic example.

John Burnside, 'History'

In the days after the terrorist attacks on 11th September 2001, the poet is on a beach with his wife and his son Lucas. The beach is on the east coast of Scotland near an RAF base in Leuchars. Above them, 'war planes' fly, presumably on training manoeuvres. The poet has a 'dread / of what may come' after the attacks. His son is rock-pooling, looking for interesting shells and fish. The family also flies a kite. Burnside reflects upon the best way to live in the world 'and do no harm'. He is sceptical of notions of race and nation states. He concludes tentatively that we should be aware of the ever-changing environment around us, and pay attention to the things which cannot be saved.

Commentary In many ways, this is the most ambitiously philosophical poem in the anthology — it asks big questions about how to be at home in the world in the face of the vast, impersonal and destructive forces of history. The poem is also located in the Romantic tradition (see the **Context** box on page 19) in its appreciation of the transient beauties of the natural environment at risk from mankind.

The title, 'History', is grand and general. It announces the philosophical concerns of the poem, but it is undercut quickly in two ways: the specificity of the subtitle (a very precise time and space) and the clear contrast with first line of the poem, which is a single word, 'Today' (repeated a few lines later). So already there is a tension at play between the general and the local.

The poet — on a beach with his family — is reminded of the dread of the wider world and the forces of history as the 'war planes' from the nearby RAF base 'cambered and turned / in the morning light'. Even a gasoline smell from the military base can be smelt 'gusting across'. Burnside, along with others on the beach, is filled with a 'muffled dread / of what may come' – global politics and nation states are shown to be intruding on the personal and the private. Interestingly, the poet – in a **symbolically** religious act – kneels down in the sand with his son in a quiet but resilient gesture. In contrast to the war planes, the poet and his family are trying to find 'evidence of life' and hope, rather than destruction. Although all he finds are fragments – 'driftwork', 'smudges of weed' and 'shreds of razorfish'.

However, Burnside argues that these fragments – things which are always changing and are 'irredeemable' – are where we must look in order to survive spiritually. Therefore the poem is threaded with such images as it embodies what it is arguing – it is being attentive to the immediate world. The sand is described metaphorically as 'spinning off in ribbons' – shifting, moving and impossible to pin down. We have also the 'distance and the shapes / we find in water', where water's formless qualities become a playful space for the imagination. The 'silt and tides' are always changing, pulled invisibly by the 'drift and tug' of celestial bodies. We are unable to live in the moment and notice the 'shifts of light' because, Burnside argues, we are 'confined' by modern notions of 'property' and the 'world we own'. Our perspective on the world is narrowed and weighed down to merely the material things that we possess or that we think belong to our nation state.

The notion of fragments finds its embodiment in perhaps the most distinctive aspect of this poem – its form. Lines are frequently short and irregular, as though they are suspended in space. Individual lines, such as 'gathering shells', 'transitive gold' and 'all nerve and line', are given a very delicate vulnerability – a sense that they will be lost in the space which seems about to wash over them. These lines are also fragments in their own right, and therefore complement the patterns of fragmentary images. The form, with the frequent line breaks working against the logic of syntax, might also suggest something about the difficulty of articulation, of what we try to 'dream about behind the names', behind the words.

Interestingly, the poem becomes more regular when it is being reflective rather than descriptive. In places, 'History' is in fact, highly formal with a regular **metre**. The following three lines, for example, are all in iambic **pentameter**:

> At **times** I **think** what **makes** us **who** we **are**
> is **nei**ther **kin**ship **nor** our **giv**en **states**
> but **some**thing **lost** bet**ween** the **world** we **own**

This is the stately blank verse of Shakespeare or Wordsworth, a traditional – historical? – form which serves as a contrast to the free verse of other parts of the poem. It is perhaps no coincidence that these reflective rather than descriptive lines are themselves exploring 'traditional' notions of a nation's history. The overall effect of these formal shifts from regular to irregular, from the complete to the fragmented, resonates with the flux and flow of the landscape being described.

Although the poem has a very physical and highly specific setting, there is also a searching, perhaps a yearning, for the metaphysical ('beyond' the physical; the spiritual). Being attentive, as the poem is, to the ever-changing (and disappearing) environment is in itself a kind of prayer to the natural world. However, the key metaphysical symbol in the poem is kite-flying. It appears three times, and helps to give the poem a cohesion. When flying a kite, their bodies are 'fixed and anchored to the shore' and also, in an interesting metaphor, 'plugged into the sky' by an invisible wind – a powerful visual symbol of the poem's search for metaphysical answers.

Children are another important symbol in the poem. The son, Lucas, represents an innocent ideal, a common idea in Romantic poetry. Burnside kneels down to join him in the search for life. But it is towards the end of the poem where the symbolic value of the child is made clear. Burnside wonders how we can live in the world and do no harm. Perhaps, he says, we should aim to (re)gain the innocence and attentive joy of 'a toddler on a beach' fascinated by the 'pattern on a shell'.

▲ West Sands Beach in St. Andrews, Scotland. Why is a beach an appropriate setting for the ideas explored in 'History'?

The tone of 'History' is pensive and solemn, and suits the overall seriousness of the poem's ideas. This relatively long **lyric** poem consists of only three sentences, which perhaps helps to establish this tone. With such long, complex syntax, our attention is drawn naturally towards the full stop (each coming at the end of a line, interestingly). The word that precedes the pause is therefore given emphasis. This full stop, this pause, is used to great effect at the very end of the poem – the syntax is manipulated cleverly as the long sentence builds towards the powerful concluding **couplet**, which beautifully encapsulates the poem's ideas:

> patient; afraid; but still, through everything
> attentive to the irredeemable.

TASK

Unless they are working within a very strict traditional form, modern poets choose where to break the line. Lines of poetry – none more so than those in 'History' – often work against grammatical structures and logic. Pick five line breaks in the poem and think about why Burnside chose to break the line at that particular point. What are the effects? Which words is the eye drawn towards? What impact does the surrounding space have? Can you detect any patterns?

You could also complete this task with any other poem in the *Poems of the Decade* anthology.

Context

'History' shows the influences of the ideas associated with the Romantic Movement (circa 1789-1837). Romantic poets such as Wordsworth and Coleridge not only admired the sublime beauty of nature, but they also looked upon it as a source of inspiration for their own poetry. In opposition to traditional Christianity, Romantic poets felt that a redemptive God, or at least a spirit, could be felt in nature. These lines from Wordsworth's 1798 poem 'Lines Written a Few Miles above Tintern Abbey' have much in common - in theme and tone - with Burnside's 'History':

And I have felt

A presence that disturbs me with the joy

Of elevated thoughts; a sense sublime

Of something far more deeply interfused,

Whose dwelling is the light of setting suns,

And the round ocean, and the living air,

And the blue sky, and in the mind of man:

A motion and a spirit, that impels

All thinking things, all objects of all thought,

And rolls through all things. Therefore am I still

A lover of the meadows and the woods

And mountains; and of all that we behold

From this green earth …

Julia Copus, 'An Easy Passage'

On a sunny day, a 13-year-old girl has just climbed up on to the porch roof of her house while her friend watches from the street below. It is likely that the girl on the roof has sneaked out without her mother's permission and she has not been trusted with the house key. The girl climbs through an open window and into the house. The two girls are also observed by a rather frustrated secretary over the road, whose head is full of various – and perhaps abortive – plans for the future.

Commentary The apparent simplicity of this poem – in which, effectively, only one event takes place – disguises an impressive range of complex methods and ideas. The passage of the girl from the sunny outside to the shady darkness of the house could be read as an allegory of the progression from childhood to adulthood. The image of the girl, who is for most of the poem poised between

TASK

The poem is about the passage of a girl from the roof of her porch to the inside of the house. It is also about the passage from childhood to adulthood. Why, do you think, did Copus give the poem its title: 'An Easy Passage'? Consider in particular the significance of the word 'Easy'.

Build critical skills

This poem has many interesting connections with Helen Dunmore's 'To My Nine-Year-Old Self'. What are they saying about the differences between childhood and adulthood? What contrasting poetic methods do the poets use?

inside and outside, embodies the concept of liminality which lies at the centre of the poem – that is, the girl is at a threshold of two states, but occupying neither. So it is perhaps no surprise that the poem contains a range of opposites: inside/ outside; dark/light; childhood/adulthood; work/play.

The form of 'An Easy Passage' matches the content brilliantly. The poem's sustained, almost slow-motion focus on a single moment finds a visual correspondence in the shape of the poem: a single stanza, with long, enjambed lines. The overall effect is of both stasis and anticipation. Copus' clever use of complex syntax and long sentences also contribute to this effect. Structurally, the poem is book-ended by two very long sentences in present tense (of 13 and 21 lines respectively), each slowing down what little action there is.

The childhood which the girls seem about to leave behind is associated closely with light and colour. Light seems to emanate from within the girls themselves. This internal source of light might suggest something about their inherent innocence and freedom. The girl on the roof is also wearing gold earrings and an anklet made of silver - the jewellery they, perhaps naively, associate with adulthood, along with the possibly garish nail varnish. All of these seem to catch the light in the same way and some help to suggest the delicate, possibly even vulnerable, qualities of the girls and of childhood in general.

The girls are contrasted with the adult world which surrounds them. The street is described metaphorically as having a menacing gaze which suggests the ways in which adult surveillance seeks to control and limit children. The mother does not seem to trust her daughter with any adult responsibilities, which in turn suggests the worry and anxiety of parenthood. The uninviting electroplating factory is a glimpse into the dreary world of work which awaits the girls. However, it is in the character sketch of the red-faced secretary where the adult world finds its greatest expression in the poem. Her head is full of future plans (evening class, the trip of a lifetime) which, we can infer, she will never fulfil. She is also reading an astrology column, another implied reference to the future. The secretary seems to adopt a critical stance towards the girls. The conversational phrases used to describe the girl's age and semi-nakedness suggests that this is the secretary's voice. She looks disparagingly at the freedom that these young girls seem to have - and the fact that they are wearing bikinis. Perhaps it is this, rather than the hot weather, that is making the secretary blush. The problems with future adulthood are also suggested symbolically in the narrow windowsill and the dangerous drop of the staircase that the girl is about to step onto.

The poem's structure is also carefully crafted. Copus takes full advantage of the opportunities of a third person narrator by describing the events from a number of different perspectives. The poem begins with the girl's perspective. We are given access to her thoughts, such as reflections on her waiting friend who she has romantic feelings for. In almost the exact mid-point of the poem, the (adult) narrator intrudes with a direct question which sums up so many of the key ideas in the poem about childhood and adulthood.

How can the girl comprehend or foresee what the future has in store? She blissfully does not know of the difficulties of her forthcoming adulthood. The world becomes less accommodating, more difficult and uncomfortable – physically and perhaps also psychologically – the older we get. This more distant viewpoint is then continued until the description of the secretary. It is from her perspective that the friend is described. The secretary looks up to see the girl and perhaps her own childhood.

The perspective and structure of the poem therefore chimes with the poem's central concerns – it moves from the brightly-lit girl to the world-weary viewpoint of the adult.

Tishani Doshi, 'The Deliverer'

This short poem sequence tells the story of an Indian newborn baby girl who is abandoned because she is not a boy. The baby is then cared for in a convent in the state of Kerala in India. The narrator's mother, the deliverer of the poem's title, is a temporary foster mother who arranges for the baby to be adopted by an American couple. The second poem in the sequence describes the foster mother's arrival in America with the baby. She hands the baby over to the adopting parents. In the third and final poem in the sequence, the girl has grown up. The poem goes back to the day of her birth and subsequent abandonment.

Commentary This shocking poem sequence has at its heart the abandonment of the daughter, but it also engages with ideas about motherhood. For such a short poem, there is a network of different parent/child relationships in the poem, each, in some way, disrupting conventional views of family: the baby's biological mother who tosses her onto a pile of other babies; the nun who looks after the abandoned babies; the deliverer who, for a short while, effectively fosters the baby as she takes her to America, and is also the poet's own mother; and the adoptive American parents. The situation in the poem is not unique or made up: because of a preference for having boys in the family, some parents in India kill or abandon baby girls (see the **Context** box on page 22). Also, Doshi's own mother did indeed bring an abandoned child over from India to an adoptive American couple.

It is one of the more socially engaged poems from the anthology as it seeks to draw attention to this practice in India. Doshi's compassion for the newborn babies and anger at their treatment is made very clear by the poem's **diction** and use of lists. As early as the third line we have the unembellished and shockingly general triad of proscribed characteristics. Consider the extended list in the second tercet as a further example.

The verbs are foregrounded syntactically by being placed at the beginning of the clause (and the line of poetry as well). The list itself implies the ongoing and pervasive nature of the events being described. The pitiless, apparently

> **TASK**
> Why do you think Doshi titled her poem 'The Deliverer'? What associations does this word have?

unfeeling process of the birth is conveyed in part by the short verbs Doshi uses towards the end of the poem: the slithering of the babies as they leave their mothers' bodies certainly has unpleasant associations; and the mothers throw the baby onto a pile of other discarded infants. Doshi also uses a macabre **pun** as life is described as being squeezed out – a pun which semantically contains both birth and death.

The diction and the form complement each other in 'The Deliverer'. The lines are short and frequently end-stopped. The tercets are terse and flinty, and the sentences are short and stripped-down. The overall structure of the poem sequence is circular, indicating the events described are ongoing and not unique. Perhaps for heightened emotional impact, it ends at the beginning, with the moment of the girl's birth. However, the brutality of the birth is tempered by the reader's awareness that the girl did survive, due to the combination of the care and compassion of the nun, the deliverer and her adoptive parents.

In the face of this horror, who or what is to blame? Our thoughts might turn to the mothers themselves who murder or abandon the babies. However, the final line complicates this as the mothers are described as trudging back home to sleep, again, with their husbands. The exhausted, numbed verb which begins the final line suggests that the mothers choose not to reflect upon the brutalising experience. Their act of sleeping again with their husbands implies a passive victimhood in both their maternal and sexual obligations – the sex is as difficult as the birth. But it is the adverb which concludes the poem, and which reminds us that the events described will repeat and repeat. The brutality of the final line is reinforced by the poem's form. The lines diminish in the lead-up to the last line: in the final poem of the sequence, there are two tercets, followed by two couplets and concluding with that painful one-line stanza. We now see the mothers as victims. The so-called 'natural' processes of sex, birth and motherhood are turned upside down by social, economic and **patriarchal** forces.

Build critical skills

How are the Americans presented in this poem? Do you think the poem is completely pessimistic about the situation described?

Context

Statistics reveal that in India, in the 20 years leading up to the publication of 'The Deliverer', as many as 10 million girls were killed by their parents either before or immediately after birth. Very often, they are killed for financial reasons – men are usually the main source of income, or they are considered to be able to do more agricultural work. In rural India, many parents depend on their children to look after them in old age: when daughters marry, they usually move away to live with the husband's family. Many commentators therefore point to the tragic consequences of a **patriarchal** society which prioritises and values men over women.

Ian Duhig, 'The Lammas Hireling'

The speaker of the poem is a farmer. He buys a cheap farm-hand (a hireling) at a fair. The new hireling has a positive influence on the farmer's cattle – he produces double the usual milk. One night, the farmer has a nightmare about his dead wife and hears his wife's voice coming from the hireling. He discovers the naked hireling caught in a fox-trap. The farmer thinks he had transfigured into a hare and back again. The farmer then shoots the hireling, who turns back into a hare, before throwing him from a bridge. In the present, the farmer tells us his herd of cattle is no longer flourishing. We discover that the farmer has been telling his story in a church, as he seeks to confess his sin.

Commentary This is perhaps the most unsettling – and certainly the most **ambiguous** – poem in the anthology. It seems to take delight in wrong-footing us, leaving gaps, refusing to answer questions. This uncertainty finds its figurative expression in the poem's frequent shifts between light and dark; note, for example, the **oxymoronic** 'dark lantern' in the second **sestet**. It is almost impossible to read 'The Lammas Hireling' without asking a number of (unanswered) questions. How did the hireling have such a seemingly magical effect on the cattle? Why does the farmer like company that knows when to 'shut up'? What happened to the farmer's wife? Why does the farmer track her voice to the voice of the hireling? Did the hireling really turn into a hare? Why did he shoot the hireling? Was he jealous? Is he sexually attracted to the hireling? Why does he confess every hour? Part of the joy of reading this macabre poem is that we can play a game, trying to fill the gaps ourselves.

We certainly cannot trust the speaker – he is an example of an unreliable narrator. The poem is a **dramatic monologue**, and the speaker is presented as having a very distinctive character. Phrases and references suggest that the poem takes place at an indeterminate point in England's rural past, perhaps the 19th century: 'a heavy purse'; 'elf-shot'; 'muckle sorrow'. We learn that the farmer is, initially at least, obsessed with money. He is pleased that the hireling was so cheap, and that the hireling helps him to make more money from his cattle. The **caesurae**, the frequent short sentences and the stark phrasing of 'knew when to shut up' indicate that he is bullish and authoritative; they also suggest the farmer has difficulty with language and expression. At the end of the poem, he compulsively and obsessively seeks confession. But he knows that he cannot be forgiven since he cannot reliably articulate his crime. Also, the poem's conclusion reveals that the farmer has changed substantially – his fixation with money and wealth is now completely gone. Instead we see him melting his money to make bullets. To shoot what, we don't know. His mind appears broken. Perhaps he is trying to protect himself from a revengeful spirit of nature.

What about the hireling? The poem's title certainly gives this character a significance. To understand his significance fully, we might need to consider him in the light of English folk traditions. The poem is very firmly located in this tradition, and in particular, shares similarities with the 15th- and 16th-century border ballads (see the **Taking it further** box on page 24). These ballads

Elf-shot: a medical condition from Anglo-Saxon times, believed to be caused by invisible elves shooting arrows at a person or animal; the farmer is saying his herd of cattle is disease-ridden and cursed.

To go the hare gets you muckle sorrow, / The wisdom runs, muckle care: Duhig says he got this expression from 'The Allansford Pursuit', a 17th-century witch chant restored by the 20th-century poet Robert Graves, which is available online. It is another text about being transformed into animals.

Heifers: young cows.

A cow with leather horns: an illusion to an old riddle; it means 'a hare'.

Casting ball from half-crowns: the farmer is melting down his money and making shot for his shotgun.

often tell stories of murder and violence, as well as characters who magically transform into an animal. Also, traditional folk songs frequently recall a pre-Christian, pagan sensibility. The hireling, who appears to transfigure into a hare, is clearly placed in this folk tradition, and is a Pan-like embodiment of nature and fertility. He certainly has an ease with nature: 'Yields doubled' under the hireling's stewardship, and 'cattle doted on him'. Perhaps the farmer is jealous of the hireling's ease (as well as suspecting him of witchcraft). And, of course, the hireling appears naked, suggesting a pagan fertility ritual or witchcraft.

Perhaps appropriately, given its historical setting, the poem adopts a traditional form. In fact, the shape of the poem is remarkably balanced and symmetrical: four regular sestets. This suggests a level of detail, control, recalling perhaps the authoritative nature of the farmer. However, this symmetry is cut across by the jarring effects of the enjambment. The apparently pleasant 'I grew fond of company' is undermined by the next line, 'That knew when to shut up'. Equally, 'Then one night' runs on to the following sestet and to the key, foregrounded word 'Disturbed'. Duhig uses the pauses brought by the spaces to build an unsettling tension.

Context

Pan is the pagan Greek god of nature, and is often associated with sex and fertility. He has the legs and horns of a goat.

TASK

What opposites and contrasts can you find in this poem?

▲ 'Oh, I shall go into the hare / With sorrow and sighing and mickle care, / And I shall go in the Devil's name / Aye, till I be fetchéd hame.' ('The Allansford Pursuit', a restored 17th-century witch chant)

Context

Hares feature prominently in folk songs, especially in stories about animal transfiguration, and they were also often associated with evil and witchcraft. For example, there was a belief that witches could transform themselves into hares, which would suck the milk from their neighbours' cows, draining them dry.

Taking it further ▷▷

Duhig is clearly positioning 'The Lammas Hireling' in the centuries-old folk tradition of English songs and tales. Duhig has said he had the 16th-century border ballads in mind when he wrote the poem. These folk songs are violent (often gruesomely so) and contain the supernatural (often in the form of ghosts) and animal transfigurations. Listen to the many different versions of the ballad 'Tam Lin' (perhaps the most famous, which was recorded in 1969 by a band called *Fairport Convention*). What qualities does it share with 'The Lammas Hireling'?

Context

On the online Poetry Archive, Ian Duhig describes the basis of the poem. When he was in Northern Ireland, a local person pointed out a house where local witches used to live and turn into hares. When the father was dying, his family was embarrassed because his body was turning into a hare. The man who told Duhig the story said he attended the funeral of the father, and he could hear the hare's paws beating on the lid of the coffin as they lowered it into the ground.

Helen Dunmore, 'To My Nine-Year-Old Self'

The speaker imagines that she is able to meet herself as a child. The poem is addressed to the younger self. The speaker reflects upon the nine-year-old's fun and energetic life, and contrasts this with the caution and care of the older speaker. The poem ends with the speaker leaving her younger self as she slowly peels a scab from her knee and puts it on her tongue.

Commentary 'To My Nine-Year-Old Self' is at once a celebration of childhood and an anguished lamentation over its loss. Dunmore crafts the poem carefully to draw attention to the differences between youth and adulthood, and the erosions brought about by time alone.

Like many poems in the anthology, the title encapsulates the ideas in the poem brilliantly. It, of course, immediately establishes who the poem is addressed to. Also, 'myself' is, literally, split by the 'Nine-Year-Old'. The poem therefore immediately calls into question the idea that our identity is unchanging; Dunmore instead suggests that we have multiple identities throughout our lives, and that we have very little in common with our childhood self.

The poem begins with a short, four-word sentence ostensibly a conversational filler. This establishes a sense of a spoken voice (the poem is a dramatic monologue as the poet addresses her nine-year-old self). The phrase is also formal and oddly tentative, and perhaps belongs to the circumlocutory world of adulthood, which would be alien to the child. But this conversational

Taking it further ▷▷

Duhig has also said that he was thinking of Coleridge's 'The Rime of the Ancient Mariner' (1798) when writing 'The Lammas Hireling'. Coleridge's poem is about a mariner who, while on a sea voyage, shoots an albatross (shown to be the embodiment of the nature spirit). He and his shipmates are subsequently cursed, and they all die, apart from the mariner. After eventually making it to shore, the guilty mariner is compelled to tell his story again and again. Conduct further research into 'The Rime of the Ancient Mariner'. What connections does it have with Duhig's poem?

Taking it further ▷▷

Julia Copus (who wrote 'An Easy Passage') interviewed Ian Duhig in a (two-part) podcast for the excellent *Writers Aloud* series on the Royal Literary Fund website: **www. rlf.org.uk/showcase/ wa_episode58/.**

Listen to this interview. What new light does it shed on Ian Duhig's approaches to poetry in general and, more specifically, the ideas that underpin 'The Lammas Hireling'?

TASK

What would you say to your younger self if you could go back in time? Do you look back on your childhood with a sadness that it is over, as Dunmore appears to do in this poem? Perhaps you will give yourself different advice?

Build critical skills

The poem is addressed entirely and directly to the poet's nine-year-old self. However, the younger self does not speak. What are the effects of this? How would the poem have changed if the young girl had responded?

TASK

Look at Dunmore's use of pronouns 'I', 'you' and 'we'. How are they used to suggest the distance between the child and the adult?

opening is also an entreaty. Sadly, the speaker is begging her younger self for forgiveness: for her decline and for all the things she has lost or ruined from her childhood.

The caesura at the beginning of the poem cracks the line in the centre and intimates the distance between the speaker and the nine-year-old, especially bearing in mind what immediately follows: she instructs her younger self to not be shocked by her presence or be so keen to leave her. There is a briskness here, perhaps a note of irritation. This is not going to be a happy reunion. The impatience and energy of the child also emerges, and is confirmed in the subsequent lines in the stanza. Note the energetic **parallelism** which concludes the stanza, creating a succession of active verbs. She is fully inhabiting her own body, and her joy and energy are barely contained. The image of the girl jumping from a height also operates on a symbolic level. This is the fall from childhood to adulthood.

Dunmore contrasts the first two stanzas. The young liveliness of the first stanza is contrasted with an adult caution in the second. This contrast is confirmed in the simply direct end-stopped first line of the sestet. This is followed by words from the semantic field of ill health as she reflects on the fears and ailments which have afflicted her in adulthood. Even the shared body – one of the few things the two have in common – ultimately signifies the unbridgeable differences between her childhood and her adult self.

It is worth noting the actions and experiences associated with childhood in the poem. With the poem's frequent lists, childhood is presented as one long, vivid morning in the summer – the discovery of small animals, eating sweets, making dens, rope-swings. It is a kind of earthly paradise, like the innocent Adam and Eve before the fall of experience and adulthood. The poem ends with a totemic image of childhood, as the younger self is left to peel and eat a scab from her knee.

This is a rich and memorable image with a direct appeal to the senses. The child is self-absorbed, living immediately in the world (rather than engaged in abstract reflections like the older self) and thankfully nonplussed by the worried-looking adult. But, like the rather sinister males mentioned, shadows lurk at the edges of this childhood. The poem ends with a rather awkward farewell and we are reminded that, despite childhood's joys, time is limited – the morning will soon be clouded over. After all, the speaker is effectively a ghost not from the past but the future – a sombre warning of what the years to come have in store.

Taking it further ▶

Helen Dunmore died of cancer in June 2017 at the age of 64. Her obituaries provide an overview of her work and interests as a writer. Read this obituary from the *Guardian*, and reflect on how it might shed light on your understanding of 'To My Nine-Year-Old Self': **www.theguardian.com/books/2017/jun/05/helen-dunmore-obituary**.

U.A. Fanthorpe, 'A Minor Role'

The speaker of the poem is seriously ill. She admits that being ill requires her to play a role in order to maintain the illusion that everything is okay. Fanthorpe also outlines the mundane realities of illness; hospital waiting rooms; listening to consultants; taking medicine; pretending to others that she is 'getting on, getting better'. The poet lists what she does when she is at home, such as finding happy novels to read, tidying up and answering the phone. At the end of the poem, the speaker affirms the value of life.

Commentary At the centre of the poem is an exploration of how we respond to illness and death. Up to the final line of 'A Minor Role', Fanthorpe is suggesting that we respond by desperately maintaining an illusion – to ourselves and others – that everything is fine. In effect, the speaker feels she is acting, performing the minor role of the title.

This conceit of acting is established in the first stanza, and returned to again at the end. The idea of acting assumes an audience – one of the reasons why the speaker feels a need to play a role is for other people. She knows she is being 'observed on stage'. The conceit continues as the speaker imagines playing the part of a servant in her own life, rather than a main protagonist. But even a small part like a servant can ruin the whole performance if the actor gets their lines wrong – if they don't act convincingly enough.

The poem therefore contains this tension between the desire to maintain an illusion and the stark reality that the performance is hiding. It is worth searching the poem for indications of the mask slipping. The illusion is described metaphorically in the first stanza as a 'monstrous fabric' – something colossal, fearful perhaps. Fanthorpe has also carefully crafted her line breaks in the poem:

> Cancel things, tidy things; pretend all's well,
> Admit it's not.

The idea of a gap between illusion and reality is given a physical form here. The painful admission that everything is not fine at all is given added poignancy through the simple, brief poetic line 'Admit it's not'. The space surrounding the line suggests that the truth of the illness is silencing the speaker: there is nothing more to say. Line endings are also interesting in this poem. What do you think is the impact of placing, for example, 'civility', 'misery' and 'yearnings' at the end of their lines?

As part of its exploration of the impact of illness, the poem makes interesting use of lists. The second stanza consists almost entirely of a list, suggesting the dull monotony of hospital visits, reinforced by the repeated -ing verbs. The metaphorical conjugation of 'misery' also results in an inevitable list. Towards the end, the items in the list are separated not by a comma or a semi-colon but by full stops. The silences are becoming more final, more keenly felt. It is as though the speaker is trying to control or repress her real feelings about illness by resorting to ticking things off, and gaining some consolation from routines.

TASK

The poem makes many references to talking, including a number of examples of direct speech (those parts of the poem are in italics). Why has Fanthorpe included so many references and examples? How do they link with the poem's concerns about appearances and reality?

CRITICAL VIEW

Some readers think that the poem is written from the perspective of somebody caring for an ill partner, rather than someone suffering from the illness themselves. Do you find this view convincing? Can you point to any evidence to support this interpretation? Does it alter your perspective on the poem's chief concerns?

Taking it further ▶▶

T.S. Eliot's poem 'The Love Song of J. Alfred Prufrock' (1915) shares some similarities in terms of tone and content with Fanthorpe's 'A Minor Role'. In the final six stanzas, Prufrock – the speaker – reflects upon the difficulties of growing old and realises that he has been playing a minor role in his own life. Read the poem and compare the final six stanzas with 'A Minor Role'.

Fanthorpe returns to the conceit of acting and performance in the final two stanzas of the poem, but her position has changed. She concludes by rejecting the performance: 'I jettison the spear' (often held by actors playing minor parts such as guards and attendants). Powerfully, the speaker also rejects thoughts of suicide, or at least giving in, in the defiant exclamation: 'No it wouldn't!' Being honest and direct wins out in the end as the poem makes a dramatic turn in the moving final stanza, which is a powerful single line of poetry:

> I am here to make you believe in life.

Build critical skills

Carpe diem means 'seize the day'. *Carpe diem* poetry is a type of poetry which realises the brevity of life and argues that we should enjoy ourselves while we can. There is a very rich tradition of *carpe diem* poetry in English literature. Famous examples include Andrew Marvell's 'To His Coy Mistress' and Robert Herrick's 'To Virgins, to Make Much of Time' (both written in the 17th century). Read these poems and conduct further research into the genre. To what extent do you feel 'A Minor Role' is a *carpe diem* poem? What do you think the poet means by 'I am here to make you believe in life'? Do you find the final line convincing?

Context

Fanthorpe includes a quotation from the classical Greek tragedy 'Oedipus Rex' by Sophocles (circa 429BC). Oedipus discovers that a man he killed when he was younger was his father. He also finds out that his wife, Jocasta, is also his mother. Jocasta kills herself. In his despair over his actions, Oedipus blinds himself. After he does so, the Chorus (a group on stage who comment collectively on the action) say it would have been better for Oedipus to die rather than continue to suffer. This reference to 'Oedipus Rex', therefore, adds to the theatrical **conceit** as well as to ideas about suffering which run through 'A Minor Role'.

CRITICAL VIEW

How might a feminist critic respond to the representation of gender and gender roles in this poem?

Vicki Feaver, 'The Gun'

The speaker's partner brings a shotgun into the house. It is initially described as resting ominously on a table. It is then used for target practice before being used to kill animals. The gun seems to have an electrifying effect on the house as the speaker and her partner feast on the animals they have shot. The poem concludes with the speaker comparing the exciting feast to the arrival of a pagan King of Death.

Commentary This poem positions itself against liberal attitudes towards guns and hunting, which perceive guns as dangerous and fearful instruments of violence and death. Feaver is in accordance with this liberal view in her initial response in the first and second stanzas of her poem; however she concludes that a gun can have an electrifying impact – the thrill of the hunt and the pleasure of the subsequent feasting. A gun can bring an intensity, an excitement and, ultimately, a celebration of life, despite (or because of) life's fragility. The poem is therefore structured along these lines – the initial fear and disruption a gun brings, followed by a delightful relish.

The impact of the gun is established by Feaver's use of form in the opening couplet:

> Bringing a gun into a house
> changes it.

The first line holds in tension the contrast between a gun (with connotations of violence) and a house (with connotations of safety). The line break suggests that the house has been disrupted by the gun. The line break creates a pause – a hesitancy – before the revelation of the second line. Our eye is therefore drawn towards the verb 'changes'; this is indeed a poem about change, the movement from fearful apprehension towards a primitive ecstasy.

The imagery in the second stanza continues the dynamic tension between the gun and the house. Feaver has said that the poem is based on the experience of her husband bringing home a shotgun for the first time after moving to a very rural part of the country. The gun is already infused with a sexual symbolism as the husband lays it on the table, the phallus-like 'polished wood stock / jutting over the edge' (note the interesting use of enjambment here). In the simile 'like something dead', Feaver is, at this point in the poem, contrasting the gun with its symbolic 'grey shadow' to the delicate life and domesticity of the house. The 'grey' contrasts with the 'green-checked cloth' of the ostensibly domestic kitchen table. The gun, a bringer of death, is disturbing and disrupting the ordinary.

Lines breaks, sentences and enjambment are distinctive features of 'The Gun'. The lines are at odds with the syntax as the sense of excess develops. The third stanza ends with a powerful, brutal short sentence as the addiction to the gun and to violence develops significantly and an ethical line is crossed:

> Then a rabbit shot
> clean through the head.

The poem becomes increasingly sensuous in the fourth stanza: her husband's hands 'reek of gun oil / and entrails' and he tramples the 'fur and feathers' of slaughtered animals into the house. The sensuousness reaches its culmination in the final line of the stanza in the remarkable simile: 'like when sex was fresh', suggesting the gun improves their sex life as it brings a youthful vitality and virility. The following, single-line, end-stopped stanza confirms what has been hinted at throughout:

> A gun brings a house alive.

▲ Death personified as a powerful horse rider, as depicted on a Tarot card.

Taking it further ▷

Listen to Vicki Feaver introduce and read 'The Gun' on the Poetry Archive website. Does her introduction and performance of the poem affect your interpretation of the poem in any way?

27

The speaker and her partner's ongoing relish is evinced in the **syndetic** pairs of -ing verbs in the final stanza as the feast is prepared: 'jointing / and slicing, stirring and tasting'. The poem's exploration of life and death is woven skilfully in to the final, rather startling image. The pagan figure of the King of Death is imagined powerfully 'stalking / out of winter woods' to join in the feast. His mouth is 'sprouting golden crocuses' – flowers associated with the life of early spring. The presence of death ultimately makes us cherish life because in death we recognise life's fragility.

TASK

In her different drafts of 'The Gun', Vicki Feaver changed the ending of the poem in interesting ways. An early draft ends by describing how bringing a gun into a house is like bringing in a skull. A later draft ends with the familiar **image** of a flower, but it is the mouth of a gun which is 'sprouting golden crocuses'. Of course, in her final version, it is the King of Death's 'black mouth' which is 'sprouting golden crocuses'. How do these early drafts help you to understand what Feaver was trying to achieve in the final version? Do you think the **image** of a gun being like a skull is more or less effective than the **image** of the King of Death?

Leontia Flynn, 'The Furthest Distances I've Travelled'

Larium: a drug used to prevent malaria (a tropical disease). Some people who take Larium suffer from serious psychiatric or nerve problems.

Greyhound: an inter-city bus service in the USA.

Krakow: an old city in Poland.

Zagreb: the capital of Croatia.

Siberian: a large region in Russia, associated with snowy wilderness.

The speaker remembers fondly travelling around the world. She enjoyed the freedom and the anonymity that travelling brought. The speaker then wonders why she no longer travels. She speculates that it might be due to an increased awareness of some of the dangers involved. The poem then shifts in focus towards a 'routine eviction' brought about by the break-up of a relationship. The small items that are left over after the end of a relationship, such as Post-it notes and sports socks, are like souvenirs. The 'furthest distances' the speaker has travelled – she realises – are not her physical journeys around the world but her emotional movement from one partner to another.

Commentary The poem's form is particularly distinctive. In some ways, it is quite regular: **quatrains** and rhyming couplets. However, the line lengths differ markedly; the third quatrain is a clear example of this. This perhaps suggests the restlessness and search for freedom that characterises the poem. The rhyme does, however, become full (and the line lengths more regular) in the final, more reflective quatrain as the speaker reaches her conclusion. The form could therefore be said to move from youthful exuberance to a more mature restraint.

The poem has a clear, two-part structure. The first three quatrains describe the exhilaration of travelling and being young; note the (ultimately misplaced) confidence in 'Yes. This is how / to live.' The final five quatrains put the speaker, now older, in a more domestic and mundane setting. The break between the two sections is underscored by the foregrounded discourse marker 'So' to indicate the development of the topic. The diction of the poem therefore shifts from the adventurous and the unusual: 'Krakow', 'Zagreb', 'Siberian', 'sherpa pass' and 'meridian', to the domestic: 'post office', 'giro', 'laundry', 'bottom drawers' and 'sports sock'.

The penultimate quatrain contains a **syndetic list** of four 'souvenirs' left over from 'holidaying' in people's lives: 'alien pants, cinema stubs, the throwaway / comment – on a Post-it – or a tiny stowaway / pressed flower'. The melancholy listing here suggests the apparently trivial and unembellished quality of these items. Given the context, however, this list also suggests a sadness regarding the developing distances between people. Each ordinary item is probably imbued with a very personal memory of a past relationship.

The poem uses a range of figurative imagery which connects cohesively with its core idea of journeys: 'like a meridian', 'as over a tannoy', 'the Siberian white [of] airports'. Interestingly, metaphors of journeys continue into the more domestic second section of the poem: 'souvenirs' and 'stowaway' describe – with added poignancy – the objects left behind after a relationship ends. Also, 'holidaying briefly in their lives' is a memorable final metaphor which conflates beautifully the two central concepts in the poem – journeys and relationships. It is a sad note on which to end – acknowledging the fragile, transient quality of our relationships with others.

> **TASK**
>
> Look again at the final three **quatrains**. What impression do you get of the kind of life Flynn lives now that she is older?

> **Build critical skills**
>
> How do other poems that you have studied on your course treat the theme of journeys? How do they compare with 'The Furthest Distances I've Travelled'?

Roderick Ford, 'Giuseppe'

The speaker recounts a story told to him by his uncle. In Sicily in the Second World War, the villagers and the soldiers are starving. They take 'the only captive mermaid in the world' out of the aquarium and butcher her so that they and the troops can eat. The villagers try to convince themselves they are doing the right thing by arguing she is only a fish. We discover at the end of the poem that the speaker's uncle was the aquarium keeper, and so would have been very much involved in the slaughter of the mermaid. The speaker is thankful that his uncle shows some signs of remorse.

Sherpa pass: Sherpa is an ethnic group from Nepal. Some members of the sherpa population are renowned for their mountaineering skills. A pass is a route between two mountain peaks.

Meridian: a line of longitude, drawn on maps and globes, between the north and south poles. The curve Flynn is describing is the curve of the Earth as it widens at the Equator.

Giro: before the use of electronic bank transfers, the fortnightly 'giro' payment was the normal way the government distributed benefit payments.

▲ 'The Mermaid', John William Waterhouse (1892). Why do you think mermaids have such an enduring appeal among writers and artists? Are they strong, active females? Do they have a dangerous sexual power over men? Do they embody loss and grief in some way?

Commentary 'Giuseppe' asks questions about the human capacity for evil. How do those who perpetrate horrible acts justify and live with their crimes? Can terrible crimes ever be justified? Should the rights of an individual be sacrificed for a collective good? Or should individual rights be protected no matter what?

In his exploration of these issues, Ford is interested primarily in the way that communities and individuals lie to themselves and others in their attempt to justify actions and assuage guilt. The villagers try (and fail) to justify the slaughter of the mermaid by dehumanising her. The tension between their self-justifying lies and their tacit acknowledgement of her humanity is perhaps one of the most interesting aspects of this poem. Note the switch from the pronoun 'she' to 'it' on the first line of the second stanza: instinctively, they acknowledge her humanity only to subsequently overwrite it. In the same stanza, this 'she/it' tension is made clearer:

> But the priest who held one of her hands
> while her throat was cut,
> said she was only a fish

The act of apparent priestly kindness and compassion is made hypocritical by the juxtaposed violence. The priest's hypocrisy is confirmed as he subsequently justifies the slaughter. The 'she/it' tension can also be found in the juxtaposition of the two lines: 'someone tried to take her wedding ring, / but the others stopped him'. And the fifth stanza – a terse couplet – contains the truth in the first end-stopped line, followed by the lie they told in the second line:

> The rest they cooked and fed to the troops.
> They said a large fish had been found on the beach.

Also, why would the villagers not eat the mermaid's head and her hands? Could it be because they are intrinsically human parts of her anatomy?

So it is not that the community is presented as intrinsically evil. Indeed, in many ways their instinct is a compassionate one. But collectively (note the range of people involved from different self-interested levels of society: the aquarium keeper, doctor, fishmonger, priest) they are shown to be able to (just about) convince themselves that their actions are justifiable. The poem is trying to understand the ways in which ordinary communities can carry out horrible crimes.

The poem's diction certainly adds to its powerful and shocking effects. It is stripped down, unembellished, almost anti-lyrical. For an illustrative example, look at the stark phrasing here:

> Then they put her head and her hands
> in a box for burial

There are no adjectives, there is no figurative imagery: just a plain **monosyllabic** frankness reinforced by the alliteration, especially of the solemn 'b' sound in the second line. The brutality of the villagers' actions is allowed to speak for itself. The simple diction also lends the poem the qualities of a fable or fairy tale. Equally, the verb 'butchered' in the first stanza is not figurative **hyperbole** – it is literally signifying what the villagers are doing. But there is one interesting use of **figurative** language in this powerful end-stopped line:

> But she screamed like a woman in terrible fear.

This simile is enormously shocking. It cleverly and compassionately embodies the issues about humanity that lie at the centre of the poem. It removes her humanity (she screams *like* a woman – she is not a woman screaming) but her pitiful fear is a human one. And, of course, it tells us that the mermaid is still conscious as they continue to butcher her.

Ford uses a framing narrative – the speaker is recounting a story told to him by his uncle. This opens up a dual perspective on the events. Giuseppe's first-hand account is wrapped in his nephew's judgemental point of view. It also allows Ford to reveal dramatically at the very end of the poem that Giuseppe was the aquarium keeper, and therefore was probably responsible for her capture and captivity, and so he must have been acquiescent in her slaughter. This might explain how Giuseppe's biased account is coloured by his self-justification – especially when privileging the arguments of the so-called experts (the priest and the doctor) to confirm that the mermaid is 'just a fish'. The poem also ends with a noteworthy word, as the nephew thanks 'God' for his uncle's apparent remorse (he refuses to look his nephew in the eye). This reference to God serves as a reminder of how far removed Giuseppe and the villagers are from God's ideal. But the nephew is thanking God – perhaps for his forgiveness. The nephew, who we can assume never had to experience the horrors of the Second World War, is also judging his uncle's actions. But the poem itself is more sophisticated than a simple condemnation; it strives to understand human responses to extreme experiences. And it is easy to judge if you have never been starving.

Taking it further ▶

'Giuseppe' has much in common with the literary genre of magic realism – magical and fantastical elements of fairy tales are mingled with the determinedly realistic (and frequently political). Often, these magical elements are simply accepted as part of the realistic world. For example, Salman Rushdie's 1981 novel *Midnight's Children* deals with India's independence from the British Empire. However, its central protagonist, Saleem Sinai, has telepathic powers as well as an enormous nose. Other examples include *One Hundred Years of Solitude* (1967) by Gabriel Garcia Marquez and *Nights at the Circus* (1984) by Angela Carter. *The Shape of Water*, a 2017 movie directed by Guillermo del Toro also has many similarities with the magic realism genre (and, specifically, with 'Giuseppe'). Read or watch any of these texts/movies, and make connections with the way Ford uses fantasy elements in 'Giuseppe'.

Context

Roderick Ford has said that his original inspiration for the poem came from a joke he had read in the introduction to a book of fantasy stories - the people of Sicily were so hungry during the Second World War that they ate all of the fish in the aquarium, including a mermaid.

TASK

What do we learn about the life of the mermaid in 'Giuseppe'? Write a creative response to 'Giuseppe' from the mermaid's perspective. For example, you could describe her experiences as a captive in the aquarium, watching all the other fish get taken out and eaten until it was only her left in the tank.

Context

Mermaids appears in the folklore of many cultures across the world. They are sometimes associated with danger, such as floods or storms. But they can also be benevolent, helping sailors or falling in love. Some aspects of mermaids in western culture have been influenced by the Sirens of Greek mythology, who sang beautiful songs to lure and shipwreck sailors. They are nearly always represented as beautiful young women. Hans Christian Anderson's *The Little Mermaid* (1837) - perhaps the most famous mermaid story - is about a young mermaid who is willing to give up her life in the sea in order to gain a human soul. In its exploration of the mermaid's humanity, Anderson's tale therefore shares similarities with 'Giuseppe'.

CRITICAL VIEW

Perhaps due to the simple **diction** and the fairy tale-like qualities of the poem, 'Giuseppe' lends itself to a number of different readings.

1 The poem is an **allegory** of the atrocities committed during the Second World War, especially the holocaust and the concentration camps.

2 The poem is a feminist reading of society, in which the patriarchy seeks to own and destroy the female and the feminine.

3 The poem is a Christian **allegory** – like Christ, the mermaid is sacrificed for the good of mankind.

Which of these readings do you find the most convincing and/or the most interesting? Write a two-paragraph critical appreciation of 'Giuseppe' in which you elaborate on and support your chosen reading.

Seamus Heaney, 'Out of the Bag'

The poem sequence begins with Heaney recalling the visits of Doctor Kerlin to his childhood home to attend to the birth of his siblings. As a child, Heaney thought the babies were miraculously brought out of the doctor's bag; he imagined Kerlin creating the babies out of 'infant parts' strung neatly in a line. The second poem in the sequence switches to the present, where the older Heaney is visiting an ancient Greek ruin at Epidaurus (see the **Context** box on page 37). He recalls taking part in a Catholic procession as a 17-year-old, and nearly fainting in the sun. Again, Heaney nearly faints among the ruins at Epidaurus. He hallucinates that Doctor Kerlin is creating babies out of 'baby bits', like a magician. In the third poem, Heaney sends off 'Bits of the grass' from the site at Epidaurus to his sick friends at home. Heaney, too, is old and tired, and wishes to be visited by Hygeia, the goddess of health. The final poem returns to Heaney's childhood and the room where he was born. His mother, who has just given birth, is described. She asks the young Heaney what he thinks 'of the new wee baby the doctor brought for us all'.

Commentary Although it is perhaps the most complex set poem from the anthology, it is an enormously rewarding one which repays repeated readings. Heaney, who died in 2013, is widely acknowledged as one of the finest poets of his generation, and his poetic craft and philosophical wisdom are clearly evident in this remarkable poem. 'Out of the Bag' covers a range of intersecting topics and themes, each cleverly echoing another: illness and medicine; class; childhood and memory; motherhood; creativity and poetry; birth and origin; religion; and the figure of Doctor Kerlin. A nexus of these ideas can be traced in many of the poem's events and images: for example, Heaney's fainting fit in the second poem suggests illness, religion (he is visited by the god-like figure of Kerlin) and birth (he emerges from his fainting fit as though he is re-born, 'blinking and shaky').

Perhaps the most memorable aspect of the poem is the figure of Doctor Kerlin. He is clearly of a higher social class than the family he visits. Note, for example, the lined insides of the mysterious bag; his 'waistcoat satin'; or the luxurious alliteration as the doctor, priest-like, holds his hands behind him to be 'squired and silk-lined into the camel coat'. In the final poem, the family make sure that, during the mother's labour, the best sheets are on the bed for the doctor. To the children in the family, this higher social class also seems to infuse the doctor with god-like powers, as though, **Hyperborean**, he is visiting the humble farm house from a perfect mythological realm.

The family attend to Doctor Kerlin during his visits with repeated rituals suggestive of a religious ceremony. In an interesting simile, Kerlin returns the contents of his bag 'like a hypnotist', maintaining the creative and religious mystery of birth as he 'tie[s] the cloth' and 'Darken[s] the door'. It seems that the role of the young Heaney and his siblings was rather like altar boys in a Catholic mass, as they prepare the water for the priest-like Kerlin. The clause 'that was next' suggests the ritual has a clearly-set sequence of actions. The water, in an example of the many phonological patterns in the poem, is 'saved for him' and 'savoured by him'. Perhaps this is due to the innocent, child-like perspective of Heaney from whom the biological aspects of birth have been withheld and the miraculous birth of his baby brother or sister could only be explained by the mysteries of faith.

To the young Heaney, Doctor Kerlin's powers could also be terrifying. The child imagines what happens in a 'locked' room during the birth. A horrifyingly gothic scene, reminiscent of Doctor Frankenstein, is described; the infant parts hung up, 'A toe, a foot and shin, an arm, a cock // A bit like the rosebud in his buttonhole'. Note the impact of the **asyndetic list** alongside the shocking conflation of the horror and charm of Kerlin in the simile in the concluding one-line stanza. Interestingly, the scene also has parallels with classical Greece, where patients visiting asclepions would bring small marble sculptures of afflicted body parts as offerings.

The diction becomes more learned in the second poem as the focus shifts towards classical Greece. The adult Heaney has become a highly educated poet, and

Context

Seamus Heaney was born in April 1939. He grew up in a rural part of Northern Ireland, and he was the eldest child of nine siblings.

Hyperborean: a race of giants from Greek mythology who lived in a perfect world, 'beyond the north wind'.

Lourdes: a prominent Catholic pilgrimage site in the south of France. Large numbers of pilgrims travel to Lourdes each year to seek physical healing.

Scullery: a small kitchen normally used for washing dishes.

Poeta doctus: a poet who (like Heaney?) is well schooled in classical models and ideas of Greece and Rome.

Peter Levi: a poet, archaeologist and Jesuit priest. He was a professor of poetry at the University of Oxford. He died in 2000, a year before 'Out of the Bag' was published.

Graves: Robert Graves (1895–1985), an English poet, novelist and classicist.

Thurifer: the person who carries the container in which incense is burnt during a religious ceremony.

moved a long way from his origins, exemplified in part by the Latinate vocabulary in the first tercet. Later, we are told that the sanctuary of Asclepius was a site of incubation, 'meaning sleep / When epiphany occurred and you met the god…'. This is another of many instances in the poem where medicine (people would visit the sanctuary to be cured), religion (the gods would provide the cure) and poetry (to be visited by a god is a moment of creative epiphany) combine and intersect.

In contrast to the vigour of Kerlin, Heaney – the modern, post-religious man – is tired and impotent while at Epidaurus. He is 'hatless, groggy' in the heat and nearly faints, just as he did in a religious procession at Lourdes when he was 17. He posts grass, plucked from the site, as a token to ill friends at home (knowing that, medically, it will not help); he wants to leave the other tourists, 'lie down' and wait to be visited by Hygeia (knowing she will not come). Modernity's faith is in science and chemotherapy, rather than the gods.

With the exception of the single-line stanza in the first poem, the sequence is written throughout in tightly controlled tercets of unrhymed pentameter. And, structurally, 'Out of the Bag' comes full circle. We begin with the child's experiences during the birth of a sibling, moving to the events at the archaeological site. Finally, back to 'the room I came from' as the self-effacing mother – who has a very real power to create life – maintains the myth of the powers of Doctor Kerlin. This form and structure lends the sequence a cohesion, appropriate and necessary for the startling breadth of ideas explored. Heaney therefore chooses to conclude this poem with the distinctive voice of his mother:

'And what do you think
Of the new wee baby the doctor brought for us all
When I was asleep?'

There is a sadness here – the mother does not want to acknowledge her own essential, life-giving significance in the birth. She is happy for Kerlin (male, educated class) to take all the credit, like the gods at Epidaurus who would visit the patient. Her authentic, colloquial diction, her simple monosyllables and considerate, warm question, mark her out from Heaney's scholarly tone. Perhaps Heaney is suggesting that it is in the local, and in the warmth of family where we might find answers to some of the poem's questions about illness, medicine, religion and birth.

TASK

'Out of the Bag' contains a complex network of ideas, each one echoes another and finds an embodiment in the poem's many events and memories. For each event/memory listed below, consider how it develops and combines ideas about **birth**, **illness** and **religion**:

- Doctor Kerlin's bag
- the depiction of the 'locked room' towards the end of the first poem
- the shrine at Lourdes
- Heaney fainting at Epidaurus
- the presentation of Heaney's mother in the final poem.

▲ The ruined asclepion at Epidaurus. It is here that the speaker of 'Out of the Bag' faints as he 'bent / To pull a bunch of grass' and where he wants 'nothing more than to lie down / Under hogweed, under seeded grass' to be visited by Hygeia.

▲ 'The Wine Glass', Johannes Vermeer (c. 1658–1660). 'A Dutch interior gleam / Of waistcoat satin and highlight on forceps'.

Dutch interior gleam: a reference to 17th-century Dutch painters, such as Vermeer (1632–1675), who specialised in painting scenes inside people's houses.

Taking it further ▶▶

Spend some time exploring this online archive devoted to Heaney. It contains many documentaries of Heaney's life and works: **www.rte.ie/archives/ profiles/heaney-seamus/**.

Context

Modern Europe has, to a large degree, separated science and medicine from religion and spirituality. However, in ancient Greece they were one and the same. Healing sanctuaries were called asclepions (the main one was at Epidaurus - the ruins of which can be visited). The Priest Doctors centred their healing around a dream therapy - patients would bathe and diet; they would then enter the sanctuary and make an offering; finally, they would enter the dream incubation chamber and fall asleep, in the hope of receiving a divine and healing visitation from the god Asclepius or his daughters.

Alan Jenkins, 'Effects'

The central action in the poem is the speaker holding his mother's hand. It is confirmed at the end of the poem that his mother has just died. He notices the scars on her hand. The hospital has removed her ring and her watch. The poem outlines distant memories of his mother when the speaker was younger, and more recent memories of his mother's deterioration brought by ill health. The speaker recalls visiting his mother in a psychiatric ward. The poem ends with a nurse bringing 'the little bag' of his mother's personal effects to the speaker.

Commentary This incredibly poignant poem outlines — with painful honesty and regret — the speaker's response to the death of his mother. The poem is carefully crafted to give the impression of immediacy. It describes the overwhelming flow of memories and associations the speaker experiences as he holds the hand of his mother who has just passed away.

The poem's syntax is a key part of this impression of a flood of memories. It consists of just two very long sentences, suggesting that each thought or

TASK

Although the poem has not been divided into stanzas, it does have an organised structure. Divide the poem up into different sections and give each section a title. The first section, for example, could be 'Mother's cooking'. When you have finished, reflect on the structure. What do you notice about the way Jenkins has put the poem together? Why might he have done it this way?

Build critical skills

Could the key figure and central focus of the poem actually be the speaker rather than the mother? What kind of man is he, do you think? What does the poem suggest about the psychology of loss and grief?

impression leads on to another. For example, noticing his mother's scarred hands at the beginning of the poem leads to eight lines of associations and memories. Later on, Jenkins uses the absence of her watch to skilfully string together a sequence of negative clauses, beginning with 'I'd never known her to not have *that* on', followed by 'Not in all the years … not when my turn came … Not all the weeks I didn't come' and so on. This sequence of negators adds clearly to the poem's overall sense of loss.

Listing – of words as well as clauses – is also a distinctive feature of the poem's syntax. The listing in the first eight lines reinforces his mother's resilience and the ongoing physical difficulties of her domestic chores. However, towards the end of the poem, the syndetic listing of verbs suggests the poignant emptiness of his mother's existence in old age:

> blinked and poured
> Drink after drink, and gulped and stared

Again, the poem's form works to reinforce the sense of the unstoppable flow of emotions and memories that the speaker is experiencing. With its single long stanza, it looks like a poem in which a dam has burst – it is incessantly refusing to pause, to accept a silence (compare this with Burnside's 'History'). Alongside this, the poem has a regular form – many lines are in iambic pentameter (or close variations), such as: 'The **knu**ckles **red**dened, **rough** from **scrub**bing **hard**'. 'Effects' is a clear example of form (order and control) being in dynamic contrast with the content (freewheeling thought-associations and memories). The speaker is trying to make sense of – and impose a structure on – this powerfully overwhelming experience and its attendant guilt. Jenkins also crafts his rhyme interestingly; some rhymes are distant ('raw' and 'drawer', for example, are seven lines apart); some rhymes are couplets ('knew' and 'stew'). The speaker admits to an ambivalence regarding how close he was to his mother – this ebb and flow of rhyme seems to say something about the nature of their relationship. The rhymes come closer together as the poem ends. What might this suggest about the speaker's relationship with his mother?

This is a painfully honest poem which kicks against the prevailing platitudes of grief – the speaker admits to not being close to his mother. Only now that she is dead is he able to acknowledge this; only now that she is dead is he able to hold her hand. Throughout his life, he appears to have adopted a superior attitude towards his parents. He says the only way his mother knew how to give love was in a 'cheap cut of meat'. Her meals are dismissed as 'Old-fashioned,' and she is resistant to new cuisines and new experiences. She belongs to a different, older generation – he thinks that his parents have lived a narrow, limited life (restrained in part by economic hardships). The son, however, has grown up and become educated. He would 'disdain' the television soaps and game shows that his parents watched; he 'learned contempt' for her as he grew up.

Not only this, but the speaker also admits that he didn't want to visit her, even when she was a widow, alone in the house. In perhaps the most moving part of the poem, her last words to him were 'Please don't leave'. But, crucially, he left anyway. The 'little bag of effects' at the end of the poem therefore clearly has immense **symbolic** significance. Has the mother ultimately had very little effect on the speaker? Is he acknowledging at the end, as the bag is brought to him, that his mother did have an effect, but he has only just realised or learnt to appreciate this?

Sinead Morrissey, 'Genetics'

The speaker looks at her hands and reflects that she is a combination of the DNA of her mother and her father. Her parents have separated but they are still 'together' in her. The end of the poem is addressed to a lover as the poet thinks about the future, and the possibility of starting a family of her own.

Commentary The premise behind this poem is a relatively straightforward one; we are each the living embodiment of our parents' union and we inherit a unique combination of our parents in our own body. The achievement of the poem lies in its skilful use of form.

'Genetics' is a villanelle, which is a traditional form consisting of five tercets followed by a single quatrain (for a total of 19 lines). The first and third lines of the first tercet recur alternately in the following stanzas as a **refrain**, and they also form a final couplet. In a poem in which the poet is trying to negotiate with her own personal past, it is perhaps appropriate that it is located in a traditional, historical form. Morrissey has also said that the form of the villanelle is the poetic equivalent of the double helix of DNA. The form certainly creates a mantra-like effect, an incantation almost, as the poet keeps returning to the same ideas.

The weaving of lines and the alternating refrain echo the processes of union, duplication and separation that the poem describes — the inheritance of genetic codes replicated in the speaker's hands. Of course, Morrissey adapts the form: the central rhyme ('palms'/'hands') is a half-rhyme. The refrains are merely similar, not complete copies: 'I know my parents made me by my hands' progresses to 'at least I know their marriage by my hands'. The speaker is not a complete copy of her parents, either.

The syntax of 'Genetics' is also noteworthy. Morrissey makes distinctive use of parallelism in the poem.

> My father's in my fingers, but my mother's in my palms.

The structure of these two clauses is the same, but the vocabulary has changed ('father's' becomes 'mother's', 'fingers' becomes 'palms'). Another example is in the second tercet: 'to separate lands, / to separate hemispheres'. This syntactical parallelism could be seen to subtly embody ideas about genetic duplication.

The speaker is all that is left of her parents' commitment to one another; they have been 'repelled' from one another and may 'sleep with other lovers'. The metaphor of her body being their religiously sanctified 'marriage register' is therefore an appropriate one. Alongside other religious vocabulary, the metaphor is extended as the speaker imitates the child-like game of making a chapel with her hands ('here's

> **TASK**
> What is the significance and impact of the rhymes and half-rhymes in 'Genetics'?

Taking it further ▶

Read the following three highly-regarded modern villanelles. How is the poet using form to match the content? Do they vary the form in any way? How do the poems compare with 'Genetics'?

▶ Elizabeth Bishop, 'One Art'
▶ Dylan Thomas, 'Do not go gentle into that good night'
▶ W.H. Auden, 'Villanelle'

TASK

To help recognise the partial perspective of a text, it is often useful to consider the narrative from a different point of view. Try re-writing 'From the Journal of a Disappointed Man' from the perspective of one of the workmen, or perhaps an objective third-person narrator. What differences arise in the alternative version?

a church, here's a steeple' and so on). Although their marriage is ended, it also continues in her, where her parents are forever unified 'where fingers link to palms'.

The structure of 'Genetics' resists the neat circle demanded by the form, however. The final quatrain takes the poem in a new direction – it becomes, effectively, a love poem. The speaker addresses a lover as she asks him 'take up the skin's demands' and start a family. 'Bequeath' is an interesting legal verb, meaning to hand down or pass on for others to inherit. The end-stopped final line is also significant:

> We know our parents make us by our hands.

This is a refrain taken from the opening tercet, and so, like all villanelles, it lends the poem a circular structure, symbolising the generational cycle the poem describes. There is an important change from the first tercet, however. The first-person singular pronoun 'I' becomes the plural 'We'. In a hopeful uplift and a widening of the lens, Morrissey recognises not just her lover but also the common humanity that we all share and we all bequeath to future generations.

Andrew Motion, 'From the Journal of a Disappointed Man'

The speaker encounters a group of workmen trying to drive a pile (a post driven into the ground to support a structure) into a pier. The speaker comments on the size and scale of the pile, the tools and the men. He realises that the men have encountered a problem which they cannot fix. The workmen stare silently at the works before walking away. The speaker is left alone with the pile, which is left suspended in the air.

Commentary This is another poem that makes interesting use of a persona. Although the poem is ostensibly about some workmen, its real focus is on the character of the speaker. With an apparent lack of self-awareness or reflection, he adopts a condescending tone towards the workers, and seems keen to maintain the social distance between them and himself.

The title is the first clue about the nature of the speaker. Its learned, faintly old-fashioned tone suggests works of fiction or diaries from the 18th century, and therefore indicates that he is well educated. Similarly, the form of the poem has deliberate associations with the past – ordered, sequential and regular quatrains, most of which are end-stopped. There is therefore a certain precision, an emerging fastidiousness to the speaker. The poem's diction also confirms the speaker as an educated intellectual as well as someone who is rather supercilious. It is **polysyllabic** and Latinate. Is the speaker – who seems a rather listless observer with nothing better to do than watch some bored workmen for over an hour – using his complex vocabulary to assert a rather unfounded superiority?

The central contrast in the poem is between the speaker and the workmen. Their language, if they speak at all, is functional, monosyllabic. They are described as strong and large men who do not appear to care either way about their failure. However, because the poem uses a partial – perhaps unreliable – narrator, it is difficult to separate out the descriptions of the men from the implied attitudes of the speaker (the poem is therefore making use of an **ironic** mode – the words do not quite mean what they appear to mean). So the men are described metaphorically as monstrous creatures perhaps suggesting the speaker's bourgeois fear of the working class. And is there a sneering, snobbish sarcasm as the foreman is described as a sort of grand philosopher? Interestingly, the rather solitary speaker remarks that the workmen were taking no notice of him. Why, we might ask, would they do otherwise?

As the title suggests, this is a poem about failure – perhaps a type of creative failure. The workmen clearly fail at their task as they slow down, then stop, then stare in silence before walking away. The speaker also fails. Despite his education, he does not have an answer to the issue at hand. Failure finds physical embodiment in the poem's imagery. Piers, of course, go nowhere. And the pile hanging useless in mid-air at the end of the poem finds its parallel in the speaker, who ends the poem with a rather listless – and faintly absurd – ignorance.

> ## Build critical skills
>
> 'From the Journal of a Disappointed Man' could be said to be exploring the concept of masculinity. What different types of masculinity are presented in the poem? How are they presented? What does the poem suggest about the nature of masculinity?

Context

```
Piers became fashionable at seaside resorts during the
Victorian era, and their sole function was for holiday-
makers' pleasure. They are regarded as fine examples of
19th-century architecture and engineering. The success
and confidence of these Victorian engineers are perhaps
contrasted with the failure of the 21st century workmen
(and the educated speaker) in Motion's poem.
```

Daljit Nagra, 'Look We Have Coming to Dover!'

The poem describes the experiences of illegal immigrants as they arrive in Britain. After a journey 'stowed' on a boat, they work in the illegal labour market, 'unclocked by the national eye'. Their hopes are to gain a passport and become financially secure legal British citizens.

Commentary Nagra has said this poem is part of his interest in the English language as a migrant language, of how it has been exported globally during Empire, and imported back through the movement and immigration of people. Despite (or, indeed, because of) its linguistic effervescence and playfulness, 'Look We Have Coming to Dover!' is a profoundly political poem, with debates over national identity at its centre.

Written in the voice of an immigrant for whom English is an additional language (the title immediately announces this), the dismantling and vibrant reclaiming of English language from its narrow, rather moribund, 'standard' grammar is playing out the wider impact of immigration on English national identity. The language sometimes used by the media to describe migrants, such as 'invade', 'teemed'

TASK

This poem is enormously rich, with many sound effects and also a real playfulness with language. Randomly select three separate lines from the poem. Identify as many methods as you can in each line. Consider some possible effects and how these techniques might contribute to the poem's overall ideas.

and 'Swarms' is reclaimed with new, rather joyful connotations. Nagra uses puns, such as the tourists 'prow'd on the cruisers'. He coins new verbs from nouns, such as 'unbladders' and 'phlegmed'. There are also a range of colloquial words and phrases with associations of working-class communities, such as 'cushy', 'hoick' and 'blarnies'. Combined, these language features represent immigrants – without any formal institutional or economic power – carving their space in the English language, making it their own. And, it seems, the English language is all the better for it.

The poem is not a simple expression of joy, however. The experiences of the migrants are shown to be very difficult indeed. They are 'Stowed' on the boat (and, later, 'hutched in a Bedford van') like an objectified piece of luggage, but also with suggestions of illegal stowaway. They feel the unpleasant 'lash' of the wind, while the settled citizens and tourists are 'lording the ministered waves'. This expression has echoes of 'lording it up' – asserting superiority – as well as a hint of government immigration bureaucracy in the 'ministered waves'. Once on land, their journey is no less difficult. They struggle up cliffs in the rain. The hazards and physical challenges are reinforced by the alliteration of the 'm' sound in 'crumble of scummed / cliffs, scramming on mulch'. They then work, 'grafting in / the black within shot of the moon's spotlight'. They live unnoticed, on the edges of society, doing the work nobody else wants to do.

But despite all of these difficulties, the speaker can imagine a future where they can settle legally and in prosperity. The wonderful coinage of using the noun 'passport' as a verb represents the central hope of the speaker and others like them. You can only be 'human' – at least in the eyes of the state – if you are given citizenship. The speaker's hopes are, ultimately, ordinary and identifiable; he wants money, a family, a car.

The poem's form, with the right margin getting narrower in each **quintet**, might visually suggest the cliffs of Dover. In another way, the lines of increasing length suggest a momentum – the gathering momentum of these 'Swarms' of immigrants relentlessly – defiantly – reaching out into Britain.

Context

Dover is a significant setting for the poem. It occupies an almost mythical status in British national identity, especially its symbolic white cliffs. They call to mind the Roman invasion; the Battle of Britain; Britain as an island nation; international trade but also separation (and perhaps difference) from mainland Europe. Dover is also the porous point of entry - as it is in Nagra's poem - and the cliffs therefore remind us that we are a nation of immigrants. The poem begins and ends with references to Dover. In a final flourish, the speaker wishes to be 'flecked' - to be a part of - the white 'chalk of Britannia'. (Interestingly, Britannia is the name the Romans gave to Britain, and has particular associations with the Victorian Empire.)

Taking it further ▶▶

Many 20th- and 21st-century novelists and poets in Britain have written extensively about the immigrant experience. Read Andrea Levy's novel *Small Island* (2004) or explore this fascinating archive of modern poems about immigration: **www.migrationmuseum. org/the-poetry-of-migration/**.

▲ 'flecked by the chalk of Britannia!' The white cliffs at Dover, with ferries crossing the English Channel in the distance. These cliffs are often the first sight of Britain for many tourists and immigrants.

Context

Nagra's epigraph is taken from Matthew Arnold's famous poem 'Dover Beach' (1867). It explores typically Victorian concerns about the loss of faith and certainty. Both poems address a lover in the final stanza. The epigraph also suggests Nagra's attempts at a dialogue with Britain's 'traditional' literary heritage and Victorian Empire. In the context of Nagra's poem, the epigraph seems to suggest the hope that the immigrants have as they set out for Britain. Arnold, however, felt that the world seems beautiful but is in fact full of doubt and suffering.

The sea is calm tonight.

The tide is full, the moon lies fair

Upon the straits; on the French coast the light

Gleams and is gone; the cliffs of England stand,

Glimmering and vast, out in the tranquil bay.

...

Ah, love, let us be true

To one another! For the world, which seems

To lie before us like a land of dreams,

So various, so beautiful, so new,

Hath really neither joy, nor love, nor light,

Nor certitude, nor peace, nor help for pain...

Ciaran O'Driscoll, 'Please Hold'

The speaker is on the phone to an automated call-centre. He is becoming increasingly frustrated by what he calls 'the robot'. Communication breaks down and he cannot achieve anything. His wife tells him 'this is the future' and that he should accept the situation. The poem ends with a suggestion that the future will be a particularly bleak place.

Commentary This poem isn't just an amusing poem about the frustrations of using an automated telephone system. It is also a darkly comic satire. Satire is a literary mode or genre in which humour is used to expose a major problem or shortcoming in society; in this case, 'Please Hold' is making a serious point about the impact of technology on our lives and the breakdown in effective communication brought about by modernity. Technology is intended to help us and make our lives easier. But, as this poem shows, this is not always the case. The speaker is reduced to an angry impotence as the technology actually prevents and restricts him at every turn. The future – which is, we are frequently reminded, already happening – is a society where language is moribund and individuals are powerless.

At the heart of this poem is the impact that technology – and perhaps the wider modern world – is having on language itself. It is a poem about the inability to communicate successfully. The poem makes frequent use of repetition (the instruction 'please hold', for example, is repeated six times). 'This is the future' functions as a nightmarish refrain (repeated five times) as his wife seems to suggest he should just accept this new world. Through incessant repetition, words tend to lose their meaning – they end up signifying nothing. Also, repetition suggests communication is operating in a kind of labyrinthine loop as language endlessly folds back on itself.

There is also a lot of syntactical repetition in the poem. Note the parallelism in these lines:

> Wonderful, says the robot
> when I give him my telephone number.
> And Great, says the robot
> when I give him my account number.

This is a 'robotic' repetition. This is what happens, the poem is suggesting, when we talk to a robot that is behaving in accordance with programmed algorithms and nothing more. The robot is saying 'Wonderful' but he – it – does not mean Wonderful. Meaning has disappeared. The speaker picks up on this in the bitterly **ironic** 'I have a wonderful telephone number'.

The poem also makes interesting use of **heteroglossia** – that is, a variety of different and competing voices within the same text. We have the speaker's thoughts, the speaker's dialogue, the voice of his wife, the robot and the speaker's 'translator'. The heteroglossia is a major contributing factor to the reader's disorientation and confusion – the nightmarish piling up of voices in one long stanza. This conversational tone is also developed syntactically through the frequent use of the fronted conjunction 'And'.

The final tercet is given significance by being separated out from the rest of the poem. By this point, the different voices are all combined together, so it is not clear who or what is 'speaking' these final lines. Individuality has disappeared. There is also a change in tone in these lines, brought about by the shortening of sentences and patterns of caesurae. The pace slows, the tone is more sombre. The triad in the first line of 'Please hold. Please grow old. Please grow cold' ushers in a note of death as the rhyme connects these concepts (hold, old, cold) together. The nightmarish, dystopian future is laid bare. A tyrannical technology will be triumphant. We will, the poem is suggesting, be caught in a meaningless conversation with a robot until we die.

Taking it further ▶▶

Many writers have expressed fears about the impact of technology. Very often, these ideas take the form of dystopia – nightmarish forecasts of the doom awaiting mankind. Charlie Brooker's *Black Mirror* is a television series of stand-alone dramas, each tapping into our unease about the possible devastating impact of developments in technology. Highly-regarded dystopian novels raising concerns about technology include Aldous Huxley's *Brave New World* (1931), George Orwell's *Nineteen Eighty-Four* (1949) and, more recently, David Eggers' *The Circle* (2013). Read or watch these examples of dystopia, and compare with some of the concerns in 'Please Hold'.

Adam Thorpe, 'On Her Blindness'

The poem describes how the speaker's mother – and her family – respond to her blindness. She confesses that she finds it very difficult indeed. She pretends to ignore her illness, or she laughs it off, by visiting art exhibitions or driving 'the old Lanchester' (a make of car). Even the speaker, just before his mother dies, forgets her blindness as he describes beautiful autumn colours. The poet concludes that her death makes her 'no more sightless, but now she can't / pretend'.

Commentary This incredibly moving portrait of Thorpe's mother and her illness explores the fiction we maintain when faced with illness (rather like U.A. Fanthorpe's 'A Minor Role'). What is it that makes us reluctant to look directly at illness and death? Why do we 'hide the fact that catastrophic / handicaps are hell'? Why do we prefer illusion to reality?

Like Ford's 'Giuseppe', the poem's diction is stripped down, literal and matter-of-fact:

> She turned to me, once,
> in a Paris restaurant, still not finding
>
> the food on the plate with her fork,
> or not so that it stayed on

This is a pared-down anecdote. Note the simple words, the frequent monosyllables, the absence of **figurative** language and adjectives as his mother's 'living hell' is described directly. Elsewhere in the poem, Thorpe uses simple listing with similar effects. Perhaps in a poem about honesty, about looking directly at difficult things, a highly-wrought lyrical style would not be suitable.

However, the poem is not entirely literal. After the colloquially affectionate 'like a dodgem' and the unembellished simile 'as blank as stone', Thorpe becomes much more lyrical towards the end of the poem. As his blind mother is dying at a hospital, he describes the weather metaphorically as 'golden' and the ground is 'royal / with leaf-fall' – connotations of wealth, richness and texture. The trees are figuratively 'ablaze' with colour. These are all intensely visual images, adding to the poignancy that his mother is unable to see and enjoy the scene being described. Or is the 'locked-in son' talking about the weather to avoid discussing his mother's final illness?

'On Her Blindness' returns to dialogue – the spoken word – throughout. This is significant because the poem is about what we say and don't say when dealing with illness and death. This idea is announced in the first couplet ('One shouldn't say it') and in hearing publicly of those heroes 'who bear it like a Roman'. On the single occasion where the truth is brutally presented ("It's living hell, to be honest") the son does not have an adequate response. The mother returns, poignantly, to the fiction at the end (maybe to save her son's embarrassment out of compassion): "it's lovely out there."

With the single-line exception at the end, the poem consists of unrhymed couplets. This form often suggests the rapid progression of one idea to the next alongside a lack of reflection or contemplation. There is also a lot of white space in this poem (the lines themselves – mostly in tetrameter – are relatively short as well). This space might recall the mother's blindness – and perhaps the truth that the family do not want to acknowledge. Alongside the frequent enjambment, it is a silence which surrounds the words and lends the lines a vulnerability, a sense of things being touched upon lightly before moving quickly on. This is especially true in the tentative final line, where the indefinite pronoun 'somewhere' adds to the fragility of the illusion that his mother is now watching over them. Even in death, the fiction continues.

TASK

Look at the two instances of parentheses (brackets). Why has Thorpe used them? What are the effects of each one?

Context

The title of the poem is an **allusion** to a poem by John Milton called 'On His Blindness' (first published in 1673). It is a sonnet in which Milton reflects on his blindness. He wonders how he could serve God and do his work without sight. The solution is made clear, however. He can serve God by being patient and bearing his affliction stoically: 'They also serve who only stand and wait.' Thorpe, therefore, is presenting a counter-argument in his poem: blindness for his mother is 'living hell' and she considers suicide.

When I consider how my light is spent,

Ere half my days, in this dark world and wide,

And that one Talent which is death to hide

Lodged with me useless, though my Soul more bent

To serve therewith my Maker, and present

My true account, lest he returning chide;

'Doth God exact day-labour, light denied?'

I fondly ask. But patience, to prevent

That murmur, soon replies, 'God doth not need

Either man's work or his own gifts; who best

Bear his mild yoke, they serve him best. His state

Is Kingly. Thousands at his bidding speed

And post o'er Land and Ocean without rest:

They also serve who only stand and wait.'

Tim Turnbull, 'Ode on a Grayson Perry Urn'

The poet is describing a vase made by the artist Grayson Perry. Depicted on the vase are young men racing their cars. Since the poem is only dealing with the people depicted on the vase (rather than real people), the poet recognises that these children will always be safe, their cars will never crash. The poet imagines the young people leading hedonistic, pleasurable lives, 'pumped on youth and ecstasy'. In the final stanza, the speaker imagines what a poet, thousands of years in the future, will think of the society depicted on the vase. Perhaps the future poet will conclude that this was a happy society which recognised beauty is relative.

Context

An ode is a type of **lyric** poem from classical Greece. Odes have a marked formality and stateliness in tone and style. They are associated with the ceremonial, and usually written in celebration or in honour of a person.

Kitschy:
excessively showy
or sentimental;
associated with
poor artistic taste.

Burberry: a high-
end clothing brand;
cheaper replicas are
widely available and
became associated
with working-class
culture at the
beginning of the
21st century.

**Buckfast and
Diamond White**:
cheap wine and
cider, commonly
associated
with antisocial
behaviour.

Donut Os: the
practice of rotating
a car in a tight
circle, leaving a
circular pattern of
rubber on the road.

Commentary In May 1819, the Romantic poet John Keats wrote a poem celebrating the beauty of a vase made in ancient Greece. The poem was called 'Ode on a Grecian Urn' (see the **Context** box on page 49). Tim Turnbull's 21st-century poem is, in many ways, an updated, modern version of Keats' ode. In this poem, however, the urn in question is one made by the modern artist Grayson Perry (see the **Context** box on page 50). The poem is therefore a conversation with the past – with both Keats' poem and the Grecian urn – and it asks a question about art and poetry: can (or should) young working-class people and their culture be a subject for artistic expression?

The form of the poem is closely and skilfully modelled on Keats' 'Ode on a Grecian Urn'; ten-line stanzas, in (largely) iambic pentameter, with long, stately sentences. Even the rhyme scheme is closely aligned. This highly traditional form is therefore in tension with the content: 'kids in cars / on crap estates', engaging in 'crude games of chlamydia roulette' against a backdrop of a determinedly modern Britain. This, of course, parallels precisely what Grayson Perry is doing as an artist: taking a classical form (in this case, a Grecian urn) and overlaying it with contemporary – often 'gaudy' – decorations of modern culture.

This tension between popular and elitist culture finds further expression in the poem's shifting tone. Its opening line – 'Hello! What's all this here? A kitschy vase' – establishes the poem's playful, conversational tone. The line also suggests a surprise – perhaps at encountering a kitschy vase in an art gallery. The poem is littered with colloquial diction, which locates the poem in a working-class milieu: 'louts', 'buff', 'geezer', 'burn-outs', 'crock'. Alongside this colloquial vocabulary, there are highly elevated, low-frequency expressions more commonly associated with high art (especially of Romantic poetry): 'evocation', 'inducing', 'speculate' and the delightfully Keatsian 'educe' (meaning to bring something out to the surface). Perhaps this dual register is most clearly embodied in the pun 'ecstasy' in the third stanza: this word appears in Keats' ode ('What wild ecstasy?'), meaning intense joy; it is also the name of an illegal drug. This elevated vocabulary brings into sharper focus another tension – the speaker is clearly an educated man who, perhaps unlike the young people of the poem's subject, knows who Keats is and what a literary ode is.

So does the speaker 'look down' on the young people? The tone, initially, appears superior and condescending. In a phrase which could be from the *Daily Express* (a tabloid newspaper), they are described as 'Burberry clad louts … creating bedlam on the Queen's highway' across the nation, 'pumped on … bass and arrogance'. But their world is also understood to be immediate, visceral, full of joy and pleasure (and also, on the vase at least, peaceful). Note, for example, the personification of the 'throaty turbo roar' and the sensuous 'joyful throb' of the music. The metaphor 'charged with pulsing juice' confirms their rather intense sexuality (and, because they are 'frozen' on the vase, they will never catch STDs). The tone shifts further in the fourth stanza. The speaker appears to be developing a more nuanced response as he recognises the sophistication of Perry's art. Their behaviour is antisocial and irresponsible, but what is the alternative? They are reacting positively to the suburban streets which they think are 'dead'. The fourth stanza concludes with the significant line:

> tranquillity, though, is for the rich.

The lens is, perhaps, widened here. The comfort, the peace – perhaps even the pleasure of art galleries and poetry – belongs to the rich middle-classes. The children's irreverent joy might be a response to this social injustice. Indeed, their actions are like a rebellious artist as they write their own 'signature' in burnt rubber on the street.

The language and tone in the final stanza change again. The poem becomes more elaborate, more formal, as it converges more closely with Keats' 'Ode on a Grecian Urn': 'millennia hence', 'galleries razed / to level dust' and 'free and bountiful'. Despite the difficulties faced in the 'real' life of these young people (poverty, drugs, STDs, car crashes, encounters with 'cops', social injustice), Grayson Perry confirms the inherent value of their lives and their culture. Perhaps future poets will admire their freedom and happiness, in the same way that Keats admires the young men and women depicted on the Grecian urn. And, who knows, future readers might say the same about Turnbull's poem.

TASK

Spend some time reflecting on the final two lines of the poem. What do you think Turnbull meant when he wrote that 'truth was all negotiable / and beauty in the gift of the beholder'? Why did he adopt and adapt the popular saying 'beauty is in the eye of the beholder'?

Context

Both 'Ode on a Grayson Perry Urn' and 'Ode on a Grecian Urn' are examples of ekphrastic poetry. An ekphrastic poem is a detailed recreation in words of a work of art. Other examples include 'In the Museé des Beaux Arts' by 20th-century poet W.H. Auden and 'On the Medusa of Leonardo Da Vinci in the Florentine Gallery' by the Romantic poet Percy Bysshe Shelley.

Shirley Temple manqué: a popular 1930s child star; manqué means somebody who has failed to become what they wanted to be.

Context

Grayson Perry (born 1960) is an English artist. He is perhaps best known for his tapestries and ceramic vases. He is also a cross-dresser, frequently appearing as his alter-ego Claire (hence the reference to 'Shirley Temple manqué' in Turnbull's poem). Upon classical, conventional forms he uses images and words to chronicle social concerns. He has also made a number of documentary television programmes, including *Rites of Passage* (2018), a series on masculinity (*All Man* (2016)) and a series on taste and social class (*All in the Best Possible Taste* (2012)). In conjunction with the latter, he wrote an article for the *Telegraph* which outlines his views on class and modern Britain (and therefore dovetails wonderfully with the ideas in Turnbull's poem): www.telegraph.co.uk/culture/art/art-features/10117264/Grayson-Perry-Taste-is-woven-into-our-class-system.html.

Taking it further ▶▶

John Keats' 'Ode on a Grecian Urn' was one of six odes that he wrote in the summer of 1819. Keats praises the urn's beauty and stillness. He admires the narratives depicted around the urn as being sweeter than words. He thinks they are timeless and speak across generations (in contrast to the transience of human life). The rather ambiguous ending seems to equate eternal truth with artistic beauty:

> When old age shall this generation waste,
>
> Thou shalt remain, in midst of other woe
>
> Than ours, a friend to man, to whom thou say'st,
>
> "Beauty is truth, truth beauty, – that is all
>
> Ye know on earth, and all ye need to know."

The British Library website has an excellent introduction to the poem: **www.bl.uk/romantics-and-victorians/articles/an-introduction-to-ode-on-a-grecian-urn-time-mortality-and-beauty**.

CRITICAL VIEW

How do you respond to the view that the representation of young people in 'Ode on a Grayson Perry Urn' is reductive and offensive?

Comparing themes

Target your thinking

As you read this section, ask yourself the following questions:

- What subjects or issues do the poems address? What ideas do they raise or explore? (**AO1**)
- What connections can you draw across the poems in the anthology in their exploration of themes? (**AO4**)
- In what ways does the process of comparing provide new insights into the poems? (**AO4**)
- In what ways might understanding more about themes open up new interpretations of the poems? (**AO1**)

Themes may be thought of as the ideas or concerns that the author addresses in the text – the topics or issues that the writer wants to explore. Thinking in terms of themes is a useful way to group your thoughts, and you may wish to subdivide a large theme into smaller sub-groups. A literary text, however, is not a simple, unilateral form of communication that seeks to transmit a straightforward message. Poems may ambiguously explore many different – perhaps contradictory – ideas, and readers and critics often disagree on exactly what constitutes a text's main concerns.

For the AS English Literature exam, you will be asked to compare two poems from the 20 set poems. One of the poems will be specified, but it will be up to you to decide on the second. The focus of the question might be on a theme. For example:

'Compare the ways in which poets present death in "Effects" and one other poem of your choice.'

So, in the exam, you will need to be able to recall which poems explore a key aspect or theme (in this case, death) and, crucially, what the similarities and differences are between them. The section on 'Responding to unseen poetry' in this guide will also cover how to compare in the A-level exam.

You will also need to be willing to engage with new themes and new slants on themes that you have already considered. The list of themes in this section is by no means comprehensive, nor is the list of the associated key poems. Also, the exam question may use a different word or phrase for the same theme.

Childhood

Some key poems: 'Material'; 'An Easy Passage'; 'The Deliverer'; 'To My Nine-Year-Old Self'; 'Out of the Bag'; 'Ode on a Grayson Perry Urn'

Frequently, literary texts show childhood to be a state of pure innocence and joy, which is subsequently lost or tarnished by adulthood and experience. In both 'An Easy Passage' and 'To My Nine-Year-Old Self', childhood is associated with pleasure, and contrasted with the anxiety and concerns of adulthood. The girls in 'An Easy Passage' are shown to be on the cusp of leaving their childhood behind. They shimmer with gold and silver, and are lit as if they have their own source of light. Similarly, the nine-year-old in Dunmore's poem is full of energy and a spirit of adventure. The final image of her tasting a scab on her tongue is an intensely physical symbol of childhood's joyful self-absorption. Adulthood in both poems, however, is full of doubt and anxiety, something to be feared. In 'An Easy Passage' adulthood is represented by the frustrated secretary, trapped in her office, dismissive and scornful of the girls. Similarly, the adult speaker in 'To My Nine-Year-Old Self' is full of fears. Ultimately, her world-weary experience is clouding the sunny morning of her youth.

'Ode on a Grayson Perry Urn' also associates childhood with 'ecstasy' (a word Dunmore also uses), and the young people are shown to be 'charged with pulsing juice'. However, unlike Dunmore's nine-year-old self, they will not grow old but will remain frozen on Grayson Perry's urn for 'millennia'. Unlike actual young people, Grayson Perry's will not need to go to work, face social deprivation, the 'dead suburban streets' and economic injustice. The issues with 'growing up' in this poem are therefore social rather than personal.

Men and women

Some key poems: 'Eat Me'; 'Chainsaw Versus the Pampas Grass'; 'The Deliverer'; 'The Gun'; 'From the Journal of a Disappointed Man'

Sexual and gender politics are a distinctive concern of 21st-century poetry. Identity is increasingly understood to be fractured and illusory, and there is a heightened critical awareness of patriarchal and colonial power structures.

Traditional concepts of masculinity are challenged in both 'Chainsaw Versus the Pampas Grass' and 'From the Journal of a Disappointed Man'. They both associate masculinity with disappointment and failure (rather than strength and success). As he tries and fails to destroy the feminine pampas grass, the hubristic speaker in Armitage's poem is roundly mocked. His masculine delight in the violence and power of the chainsaw is woefully misplaced. On the surface, Motion's poem seems to offer two versions of masculinity – the erudite speaker and the earthy workmen. These two masculinities equally fail. The hopeless task defeats the workers, and the educated speaker doesn't understand and is left metaphorically hanging, useless 'in mid-air'.

Other poems are from a female perspective, and seek to highlight and question gender inequalities. The speaker in 'Eat Me' is subjected to the controlling and sexualised male gaze of her partner. The final lines in 'The Deliverer' reveal that the mothers, who are forced to repeatedly have sex with their men, are themselves victims of a patriarchy which repeatedly forces them to both passively 'lie down' for their men and to discard female babies. However, some poems such as 'The Gun' might be less critical of traditional gender roles, and can therefore lead to interesting comparative responses.

Violence and transgression

Some key poems: 'Eat Me'; 'Chainsaw Versus the Pampas Grass'; 'The Deliverer'; 'The Lammas Hireling'; 'The Gun'; 'Giuseppe'; 'Look We Have Coming to Dover!'

When reading a poem that appears to present some kind of transgression (crime, misbehaviour, etc.), it is often worth considering what the poem's attitude towards the transgression actually is. Does it celebrate or condemn the act? Or perhaps the poet is more ambivalent? Does it point to wider social causes or consequences (such as 'Look We Have Coming to Dover!')? Or maybe the angle is more private (such as 'The Lammas Hireling')?

Perhaps he shot the hireling; perhaps the hireling was a warlock. In 'The Lammas Hireling', the precise nature of the speaker's crime (or crimes) is in doubt, partly because the speaker seems unable to frame it with language, and partly because of the supernatural influence of folk songs on the poem. The farmer's guilt, however, is made plain – he is condemned to confess endlessly. In the same way, Uncle Giuseppe's guilt over the mermaid's murder is made clear by the end of the poem, despite his attempts to justify it. Ford's poem is an examination of guilt – both personal and collective – and the lies we try to tell ourselves to justify transgressions. On the other hand, 'The Gun' seems to relish in the transgression. Both the speaker and her partner soon indulge in an almost primitive delight in the death that it brings – a 'gun brings a house alive'.

Past and present

Some key poems: 'Material'; 'History'; 'To My Nine-Year-Old Self'; 'The Furthest Distance I've Travelled'; 'Out of the Bag'; 'Ode on a Grayson Perry Urn'

Sometimes the contrast between the past and the present is personal, such as in 'To My Nine-Year-Old Self'; sometimes the contrast is more general, exploring social concerns or the broad sweep of history, such as Burnside's 'History'. Ros Barber's 'Material' perhaps touches upon both, as the poem outlines how larger changes in society and a lost way of life have had an impact on the way that the speaker raises her own children.

There are different versions of the past in 'Out of the Bag'. Heaney remembers his own childhood, his mother and the visits of Doctor Kerlin. The poem also references a more distant classical Greece, especially the sanatorium at Epidaurus and the ways in which the ancient Greeks would seek to be healed by being visited by the gods. In the present, Heaney is elderly and rather frail. Despite the massive sweep of histories in 'Out of the Bag', the poem is remarkably cohesive. Everything is shown to be connected through recurring motifs and commons ideas of healing and birth. Conversely, Burnside in 'History' argues that we should turn away from history as any kind of solution – at least, the grand narratives of national histories. Such histories lead to conflict and war. Instead, we should focus on the present and the personal, to attend to the moment as it happens.

Other poems explore more obviously the gap between a poet's own past – normally childhood – and the (frequently disappointing) present of adulthood. In 'The Furthest Distances I've Travelled', the speaker's past was one of exotic journeys and adventures. Her present is seemingly more mundane – as she stuffs 'smalls / hastily into a holdall' for some laundry – and rather sad, as she separates from her lover. However, the contrast between past and present is not as simple as this. The poem ends with the metaphysical consideration that the journeys she takes 'between people' are far greater and far more meaningful than her exotic trips around the world.

Taking it further ▶

Think of other texts you have read or studied on your English Literature course. Do they also explore the theme of appearance and reality? Can you identify any connections with some of the poems in *Poems of the Decade*?

Truth and lies

Some key poems: 'The Lammas Hireling'; 'A Minor Role'; 'Giuseppe'; 'On Her Blindness'

The gap between appearance and reality is a very common concern in literature. Language is often at the heart of this theme – it can be used to disguise and mislead as much as to reveal and communicate. The lies the doctor and priests tell in 'Giuseppe' hide their guilt. The speaker in 'A Minor Role' feels the social pressure to use (spoken) language to maintain the 'music of civility'. Similarly, 'On Her Blindness' speaks of our reluctance to openly and honestly discuss illness. This theme could also lead to a wider discussion of ambiguity of poems, the slippery nature of truth itself (for example, in 'The Lammas Hireling' and 'Please Hold').

Family and motherhood

Some key poems: 'Material'; 'The Deliverer'; 'Out of the Bag'; 'Effects'; 'Genetics'; 'On Her Blindness'

A number of the set poems from *Poems of the Decade* are remarkably honest and moving accounts of the speakers' relationships with their parents – specifically their mother.

Motherhood is a particular concern in 'Material'. Barber's mother is shown to belong to a vanished world of handkerchiefs and headscarves. The portrait is an affectionate one. She would always have a hanky – a soft maternal symbol in the poem – 'up her sleeve'. Barber's own approach to motherhood is contrasted; she doesn't even keep a packet of disposable tissues in her bag. However, Barber concludes by imagining her mother dispensing sage advice: the world has changed away from handkerchiefs and Barber must make the most of the modern 'material'.

Although it has a similar affectionate tone, 'Genetics' presents a much deeper connection between the speaker and her parents. She is the literal embodiment of both her mother and her father. Despite their separation, their marriage continues in her – 'My body is their marriage register'. On the other hand, 'The

Deliverer' paints a very different picture of motherhood. This uncomfortable poem forces us to examine – perhaps question – ideas about the so-called 'natural' processes of birth and motherhood. The biological mothers – dictated by their husbands and the patriarchal communities – are forced to abandon or kill their baby daughters. The poem is not without hope, as the dynamics between child and parent are radically re-cast through the nurture and care of the nun, the deliverer and, eventually, the adoptive parents. Other poems, such as 'Effects', likewise resist the cliché of the so-called unbreakable bond between child and mother. It is, as always, complicated.

Society

Some key poems: 'History'; 'The Deliverer'; 'Giuseppe'; 'Out of the Bag'; 'From the Journal of a Disappointed Man'; 'Look We Have Coming to Dover!'; 'Please Hold'; 'Ode on a Grayson Perry Urn'

This is a broad theme which can be further sub-divided. However, a number of poems highlight social inequality, none more so than 'Look We Have Coming to Dover!'. The immigrants' journey is difficult; the 'yobbish' rain symbolically 'unbladders' on them. They then work in the black labour market in the hope of somehow gaining citizenship and a settled life. They are contrasted with the 'prow'd' tourists on their cruisers. However, the poem's playful, inventive language represents the counter-influence that the immigrants have on an established, post-Imperial Britain. The hedonism of the children described in 'Ode on a Grayson Perry Urn' may be explained by a similar disenfranchisement from mainstream British society. The poem's ultimate celebration of the children as an apt subject for art is a radical alternative to prevailing attitudes which seek to dismiss or sneer.

Powerlessness is at the centre of 'Please Hold' as well, although it is the impotence of an individual rather than a group. Although maintaining a humorous tone (like Turnbull and Nagra's poems), 'Please Hold', however, is less concerned with social injustice and more with an existential crisis brought about by modern technology.

Death and illness

Some key poems: 'The Lammas Hireling'; 'A Minor Role'; 'The Gun'; 'Out of the Bag'; 'Effects'; 'On Her Blindness'

Many poems which explore the impact of death and illness are interested in the ways in which we maintain illusions and appearance. 'A Minor Role' is an account of the boredom and fear of illness. It suggests a wider refusal in society to fully acknowledge death and dying. 'On Her Blindness' is also concerned with how to speak truthfully about illness in the face of societal pressure. Perhaps unsurprisingly for 21st-century poems, hardly any poems seem to explore the metaphysical aspects of death such as ideas about heaven or the soul. 'On Her Blindness' acknowledges that the mother might be 'watching, somewhere',

TASK

Work through each poem in *Poems of the Decade*, making notes on each of the themes that it explores. You might like to make a concept map for each poem's themes, or to make one on a page large enough for you to include all of the poems' titles and to trace thematic connections between them.

while simultaneously acknowledging this as a fiction. 'Effects' is even starker – the mother dies alone in a psychiatric ward. All that is left is her son's guilt and a 'little bag of her effects'.

> ## TASK
>
> Other themes and issues which arise from the set poems in *Poems of the Decade* include, but are not limited to:
>
> - journeys
> - power
> - loss
> - language
> - class
> - sex and relationships
> - nature / the environment
> - domestic
> - guilt.
>
> Which poems explore each of the above themes/issues? How do the poems compare in their treatment of the theme? Can you think of any other themes not covered above or in the main body of this section?

Comparing poets' methods

Target your thinking

As you read this section, ask yourself the following questions:

- Consider the different methods that the poets use in *Poems of the Decade* – which are the most important or successful, and how are they used to shape meaning and to create effects? (**AO2**)

- As you consider methods and meanings, how can you use literary terminology to help you to articulate your responses with more precision and concision? (**AO1**)

- How might your understanding of the methods that the poets use help you to make connections and comparisons between poems from the anthology? (**AO4**)

In both the AS and A-level exam, you will need to show a detailed appreciation of the different methods the poets use to communicate meanings. Method is a broad concept, but includes aspects such as form, imagery, sound effects and structure. Comparing methods should always be at the very heart of your exam response.

The exam question may explicitly ask you to compare a particular aspect of the poets' craft:

'Compare the ways in which poets use imagery in "History" and [one other poem].'

The list of methods in this section is indicative and is by no means comprehensive. Further detail on methods can also be found in the **Poems and poem commentaries** section.

Humour

'Chainsaw Versus the Pampas Grass' adopts the mock-heroic form, where a simple action is described using exaggerated epic images and vocabulary. The reader is therefore encouraged to laugh at the absurdity of the speaker and his (masculine) pride. However, the humour in 'Look We Have Coming to Dover!' mostly arises from the poem's playfulness with language – its frequent puns and coinages express the vibrancy and hope of the immigrants. The humour in 'Please Hold' is also used to make a serious point – through the impotent speaker's comically extreme anger and frustration, the poem is able to satirise the modern age's dependence on technology and the resulting vacuity of the English language.

First person narrators

In some poems, the speaker and the poet are closely aligned. For example, we are encouraged to believe that the speaker in 'Effects' is largely Alan Jenkins himself. In some cases, there is also an assumed 'reader' (or **addressee**) of the poem, such as the priest in 'The Lammas Hireling'. Awareness of this intended addressee can shed an interesting light on a poem.

In a number of other poems in *Poems of the Decade*, the speaker is clearly meant to be understood as separate from the poet. This is when the poet is using a persona (from the Latin meaning 'mask'). In such cases, the attitudes and perspective of the speaker are not necessarily those shared by the poet. A persona therefore becomes a constructed literary character. Poems such as 'Eat Me', 'The Lammas Hireling' and 'Giuseppe' make a clear use of a persona. In Duhig's and Ford's poems, the narrators are unreliable because they do not tell us the whole truth. Both poems explore guilt in some way, and therefore this avoidance and obfuscation is part of the poems' attempts to understand human responses to violent transgressions. The use of a framing narrative in 'Giuseppe' – a poem about judgement and perspective – establishes a doubling of the critical distance. Ford creates a persona whose uncle tells a story about a mermaid; we therefore have the nephew's judgement wrapped around Giuseppe's attempts at self-justification. In other poems, this critical distance between the poet and the speaker is much more ambiguous. To what extent can the speaker in 'From the Journal of a Disappointed Man' be separated from the highly educated poet Andrew Motion? Do you think Armitage himself used a chainsaw to destroy some pampas grass in his garden?

Taking it further ▶

Many poems in *Poems of the Decade* belong to the genre of lyric poetry. The origins of lyric poetry can be traced to Ancient Greece, where poems were sung to the accompaniment of a *lyre*, a string instrument. Lyric poems are therefore musical, and are relatively short and non-narrative. They express the mood or thoughts and feelings of the speaker, although the extent to which the speaker is the same as the poet is often open to debate. Lyric poetry has become by far the most common genre of poetry in the 20th and 21st centuries.

Lyric poems can often be distinguished from narrative poems. These poems recount stories, and have a clear sequence of events which usually involve defined characters.

Which poems in the anthology can you confidently identify as 'lyric' poems? Which do you think are narrative poems? Are there any poems which seem to resist either of these labels, or belong to both? What makes these poems problematic?

You can discover more about the lyric and narrative genres of poetry online.

Form

Of course, all of the poems in the anthology use form in varied and interesting ways – it is arguably a defining characteristic of poetry itself. However, you should try to consider form in relation to the poem's meanings and ideas. Sometimes, form works alongside the content such as the fragmented lines in 'History' – a poem about the significance of fragments and impermanence. Sometimes there is a tension or a stark contrast between the form and the content, such as in 'Eat Me' or 'The Lammas Hireling', where the form tries to control the excess or the chaos.

Some poems use traditional forms. Perhaps unsurprisingly, the learned speaker in 'From the Journal of a Disappointed Man' is associated with the traditional quatrain. The villanelle form in 'Genetics' is highly appropriate for the poem's interest in the replication of DNA through generations. 'Ode on a Grayson Perry Urn' uses Keats' version of an ode to explore modern concerns in the same way that Grayson Perry is using classical Greek forms in his pottery.

Other poets are more experimental, such as Nagra's successive increase in line length to suggest a gathering power and momentum of the immigrants, or Flynn's rhyming quatrains, which barely hold together in the face of the restless search for freedom that characterises the poem.

Imagery

'Imagery' is simply words and phrases that summon sensory perceptions in the reader's mind. The images can be literal, such as the gun's 'long metal barrel' and its 'grainy polished wood stock' in 'The Gun'. Imagery can also be figurative (that is, the use of similes, personification and metaphors), such as the violent personification of the chainsaw in Armitage's poem. Most poems use imagery in some ways, although some much more than others. Poems like 'Giuseppe' and 'On Her Blindness' rarely use figurative devices, which adds to the stark, direct tone of these poems.

Some poems use patterns or clusters of imagery. For example, 'Eat Me' contains patterns of maritime and exotic imagery to perhaps suggest the poem's colonial concerns. 'An Easy Passage' uses recurring images of light and shade to hint at the girls' movement from the joyful innocence of childhood to the anxiety of adulthood.

Build critical skills

Rather than simply focusing on features that are obvious, select those that are most significant to the poem overall, and those most relevant to the question you are answering.

A strong English Literature essay will also explore patterns across the poem rather than a single example. Therefore, rather than just analysing the personification of the pampas grass that 'swooned' in Armitage's poem, you could locate this image as part of a wider pattern of the feminisation of the pampas grass in the poem, in opposition to the brutal masculinity of the personified chainsaw.

Build critical skills

Use a good guide to literary terms to discover more about poetic methods. Both the Oxford and the Penguin dictionaries of literary terms are very comprehensive.

Sound effects

More so than in other literary forms, poetry has an inherent musical quality. Sound effects can be significant in establishing the emotional resonance of the poem. Hearing a poem read out loud can add a whole new layer of pleasure and understanding to the reading experience.

Poets can use clusters or patterns of sounds (such as alliteration, assonance and rhyme) to reinforce tone and meaning. The alliteration and assonance in 'Eat Me', such as 'my broad / belly wobble, hips judder like a juggernaut', amplify the venality and sexual excess. These sound effects also contribute to the poem's darkly comic tone. These could be compared with Heaney's assonantal 'nosy, rosy, big, soft hand of his', which helps to establish the child-like perspective on Doctor Kerlin.

Rhyme (and half-rhyme) is also often a key part of a poet's craft. It can link opposites by sound, such as Barber's 'knitting wool' of her mother's generation and modern 'malls'. It may reinforce a similarity between two words, such as Jenkins' 'scarred' and 'scrubbing hard'. Rhyme can be humorous as well, such as Barber's 'not' and 'snot' or Turnbull's colloquial 'knocked out' and 'louts'. Poets also use rhyming couplets (and triplets) to create a strong, memorable conclusion to a poem, such as Jenkins' moving triplet at the end of 'Effects' – 'she', 'see' and 'me'; or Flynn's memorable rhyming couplet: 'What survives / of holidaying briefly in their lives'.

Sometimes, of course, the sound effect might be accidental, or included solely for its musical effects. Alliteration and rhyme can therefore sometimes be difficult to analyse meaningfully. Only choose examples that you can successfully link to the poem's meaning in some way.

TASK

Other significant methods used in the set poems in *Poems of the Decade* include, but are not limited to:

- line breaks and line length
- **ambiguity**
- syntax
- structure
- tone
- the title.

Which poems make significant use of these methods? How do the poems compare in their use of the same method? Can you think of any other methods not covered in the list above or in the main body of this section?

Responding to an unseen poem

Target your thinking

As you read this section, ask yourself the following questions:

- How do you develop a detailed critical understanding of the ideas and meanings of an unseen poem? (**AO1**)
- How do you successfully analyse the methods used in an unseen poem? (**AO2**)
- How can you use literary terminology to help you to articulate your response to an unseen poem with precision and concision? (**AO1**)
- In what ways can you compare an unseen poem with the set poems from *Poems of the Decade*? (**AO4**)

Reading an unseen poem

The singularly most effective way to prepare for an exam question on an unseen poem is to read a lot of poems. You will, of course, have read and studied the anthology – the skills and knowledge you developed in your study of these poems will be enormously useful for your reading and analysis of an unseen poem. To build your confidence and skills, you should also read a range of other poems regularly, especially poems written in the 21st century. The **Taking it further** section at the end of this guide provides you with a number of suggested poetry anthologies and websites. Remember, reading a poem once could only take a few minutes. There are many, many great poems out there, just waiting to be read and enjoyed!

Furthermore, the 'Introduction' to this guide provides you with a detailed overview of how to read a poem, and what to look out for when considering poets' methods. It reminds you that a poem is not a maths equation to be 'solved' and that you should tolerate uncertainty and expect ambiguity.

Read the unseen poem carefully and with an open mind. If you are unsure about a word or phrase in a poem in the exam, you should simply ignore it. Focus on the aspects of the text that you are more confident with, and use these to support your critical appreciation. And, because a poem only takes a minute or two to read, you should read it multiple times, even under exam conditions.

Read both questions carefully and make sure that you read the unseen poem (and the two set poems as well) before you make a decision. Do not rush this part of the process. It is better to spend time making the right decision at the beginning rather than changing your mind halfway through.

The following sections will provide you with a suggested process for responding to an unseen poem under timed conditions.

> **TASK**
> Keep a brief reading diary of the poems you read. Note down what you consider to be the main concerns, significant methods and connections with any of the 20 set poems from *Poems of the Decade*. You could then use this diary to construct and answer your own exam questions.

- ◥ **Establishing a response**: reading the poem for the first time and noting your first impressions.
- ◥ **Establishing an interpretation**: reading the poem again to develop an overall interpretation, especially in response to the exam question.
- ◥ **Developing a response**: exploring in detail the methods used and how they link to ideas and meanings.
- ◥ **Making comparisons**: considering how the poem connects to the set poem from *Poems of the Decade*.
- ◥ **Planning a response**: organising your ideas into a well-organised, comparative essay which develops an argument and answers the question.

Hollow

He was a dent in the sofa,
hollowed to fit in the corner;
at the other end, two dips: heels left in felt.

We could not fill these cavities.
Only his stoop might –
elbows sagging into cushions each morning.
We sat in other places,
avoided shadows cast
by our father.
He left himself behind, dwindled
to blank eyes, trembling hands.

Fearing the January cold
he bound the living room round with heat
thick as boiled wool, tight at the neck.

"I'm sorry," he said, "so sorry."
Our chatter tried to fill his gaps.
We edged through days, orbited empty space
of absence.

Our mother stacked his walking boots
under stairs.
His overcoat hung in the dark,
velvet collar waiting for a warm body
to fill it up.

He tried to fold himself away,
but could not curl small enough
to pass unseen.

Dust settled as days passed, months marked by
deeper hollows until, with such slowness
of bare twigs edging into leaf,
cool air spooled the house.

Upholstery dents receded.
We pulled on coats, slipped feet in boots,
and took small steps
imprinting softly into hills.

Rosalind Jana

From *Branch and Vein* (New River Press, 2017)

A possible exam question could be:

'Read the poem "Hollow" by Rosalind Jana and re-read "Effects" by Alan Jenkins. Compare the methods both poets use to present the loss of a parent.'

> ## TASK
>
> Complete this exam-type question yourself under timed conditions. Give yourself 75 minutes. Then read the rest of this section. Go back to your initial response and make a note of strengths and any areas for development.
>
> You could also evaluate your own process for responding to an unseen poem: can the process be improved in any way? Did you spend enough time planning? Did you understand the unseen poem confidently? Were you able to finish in time? Did your plan include comparative points? Were you able to remember any points from when you studied 'Effects'?

Taking it further ▶▶

The following poems all have meaningful points of comparison with 'Hollow'. For each poem, identify the point(s) of comparison. You could then construct and answer your own exam-style questions, using the question provided above as a model.

▶ 'The Deliverer'
▶ 'Material'
▶ 'A Minor Role'
▶ 'Genetics'
▶ 'On Her Blindness'

TASK

Try answering these questions on 'Hollow' before reading the following section. You can then compare your answers to those given.

You could also practise answering these questions on any other poem you read.

Establishing a response

After you have chosen the question, you should then read the poem carefully again, in order to establish and confirm your initial impressions and ideas. The questions below can be applied to any poem, and can be used as prompts to help you with your initial ideas and annotations. Remember, your answers to these questions at this early stage in the reading process will be tentative. Do not force any answers if none are forthcoming. You may also want to note down any initial connections with the set poem from the anthology (in this case, 'Effects').

The following sections will answer these questions on the poem 'Hollow', on page 62.

1   What are the effects or connotations of the title?
2   What happens? Is the poem based on a particular object, memory, person or place?
3   Who is speaking? Is it possible to work out who the poem is addressed to?
4   Is there anything distinctive about the overall form or shape of the poem?
5   What is the tone?
6   What ideas or concerns does the poem seem to engage with?
7   Are there any other (potentially) interesting or significant features? Or perhaps any questions or uncertainties to consider for subsequent readings?

What are the effects or connotations of the title?

The title of this poem is particularly rich in associations – the word 'Hollow' provides a figurative indication of the main concerns of the poem. 'Hollow' suggests not only emptiness but also an absence – something is not there that should be. It also might indicate something without substance or value (as in 'hollow victory'). In this poem it describes, on one literal level, the 'cavity' left in the sofa by the father. However, it might also link to some of the ideas in the poem about death and absence, and the speaker's father becoming increasingly insubstantial as he tries to 'fold himself away'.

What happens? Is the poem based on a particular object, memory, person or place?

This appears to be a poem about the speaker's father, primarily, with a particular focus on the shape he left in the sofa. The speaker describes the distinctive way he sat – or lounged? – on the sofa, and how perhaps in illness, he preferred the living room to be very hot. Although it isn't made clear, we should assume that the father dies: the references to 'empty space' and 'absence' suggest this. Also, the speaker's mother packed the father's clothes away. The end of the poem describes the family going out for a walk.

Who is speaking?

The daughter is narrating the events. Since she is describing her father, we might assume this poem to be rather private and personal, perhaps emotional. The poem does not appear to be obviously addressed to anybody, although the plural pronoun 'we' might suggest she is speaking, in part, on behalf of the rest of the family (and implies that she has at least one sibling).

Is there anything distinctive about the overall form or shape of the poem?

The poem is in free verse: it is not regular or formal. There is no rhyme scheme. Many stanzas and lines are rather short: perhaps suggesting something tentative, something not being said. The poet also appears to be using line breaks and enjambment to draw attention to key words and to the silence and the space.

What is the tone?

The tone is certainly serious, perhaps even solemn (appropriate for the subject matter?). There are lyrical flourishes as well, especially towards the end, where the tone seems to lighten somewhat.

What ideas or concerns does the poem seem to engage with?

'Hollow' seems to engage with ideas around death, specifically the way in which the speaker and her family respond to the death of the father. In life, he appears to exert a lot of influence over the family. Perhaps the reference to the overbearing heat of the living room might suggest this influence is not always positive. There also appears to be an interest in the poem in communication, or lack of it, as the family come to terms with the absence of the father.

Are there any other (potentially) interesting or significant features? Or questions or uncertainties to consider in subsequent readings?

The final images are interesting – the cool air entering the house and the family heading out for a walk, leaving soft imprints. Are they finally able to walk away from the overbearing father? Or is it just an image of them coming to terms with his death? Does the 'presence' of the father cast shadows because of his domineering nature or because he is dying? Also, the image of the impression left in the sofa has a central significance in the poem, and links to the title and the idea of absence.

Establishing an interpretation

After your initial response, you should read the poem again in order to develop an overall interpretation. This will require you to read the text carefully, and identify what its (often implied) meanings or perspectives are in relation to the focus in the question.

'Read the poem "Hollow" by Rosalind Jana and re-read "Effects" by Alan Jenkins. Compare the methods both poets use to present the loss of a parent.'

Therefore, the focus of this exam question is on Jana's presentation of the loss of the father. Different readers will develop different interpretations, emphasising different aspects of the poem, or prioritising a particular image or stanza over another.

In 'Hollow', you may have picked up on the speaker's ambivalence towards her father. This is not a straightforward poem about grieving a loved one. Jana is implying that the loss of a parent is complex, full of contradictions and uncertainties. Parents – being human – have flaws and shortcomings.

For example, the line 'We could not fill those cavities' is ambiguous: is the speaker merely outlining the unique, distinctive shape of her father's body? Or are the speaker and her siblings prohibited from sitting in their father's 'seat'? And do the 'shadows cast' by the father suggest his dominance? Or do they imply the family's fearful reluctance to confront his (imminent?) death? However, the father, in illness, is also a forlorn figure, evoking sympathy. He 'left himself behind' and wants to disappear and 'pass unseen'. Also, he apologises: '"I'm so sorry"'. But, we might ask, for what? The end of the poem, as the family head out tentatively for a walk, might suggest they have come to terms with the death of the father. Or perhaps they are now able to enjoy life now he that has passed on?

Developing a response

You then need to develop a more detailed response in order to answer the exam question fully. You therefore need to read the poem at least one more time. The focus should now be on how the poet has used a range of methods to present their ideas in relation to the question. This will probably require detailed annotations.

You will need to apply your knowledge of the distinctive aspects of poetry that you have been developing on your A-level course. You could consider the poem's **structure**, **diction**, **imagery**, **form** and **sound effects**. This list, however, is by no means complete. In any case, you should certainly avoid mechanically applying any kind of 'checklist'. Not all items in a list will be relevant for all poems – some poems, for example, may have no imagery in them at all. You must always be sensitive to the ideas and the distinctive qualities of the poem. Meanings – especially those which relate to the focus of the question – should be at the centre of your response. It can be very easy to spot alliteration or a simile, but a successful literature student will be able to consider how these methods are used to suggest or reinforce meanings and ideas.

TASK
Read through 'Hollow' again and note down any potentially interesting poetic methods. After you have completed this, go on to read the suggested points provided here, and add (where appropriate) to your own notes and annotations. Are there any significant differences between the methods you identified and those identified in this section?

Some significant methods in 'Hollow'

- **The vocabulary of loss**. Threaded through the poem are a number of words which relate to loss and absence: 'hollowed', 'cavities', 'blank', 'gaps', 'empty space', 'absence', 'deeper hollows'. The father's death is imagined as a disappearance, a hollow felt by the family – conversely – as a presence, almost haunting the living room.

- **The change in focus and tone at the end**. Like the family, the poem mournfully orbits the 'the empty space / of absence', structurally circling around the loss. However, the final two stanzas describe a passage of time, and suggest (perhaps metaphorically) the arrival of spring. The tone softens slightly; the family have finally learnt to break free of the orbit of loss as they step out. The mood literally lifts up as they ascend the hills.

- **Line breaks and enjambment**. Free verse provides perhaps more opportunities for a poet to break a line at key points, and to vary the use of space. The lines in 'Hollow' are frequently short, creating a space around the words – space which suggests the poem's subject: absence. The short lines 'of absence', 'to fill it up' and 'to pass unseen' certainly confirm this. The line break in 'shadows cast / by our father' is also, in a way, casting a shadow of its own. Many of the words associated with loss (see above) are also placed at the end of the line, and therefore are proceeded by pauses and gaps.

- **Figurative imagery**. The image of the imprint left in the sofa is used figuratively: the father is described metaphorically as a 'dent in the sofa' and the dents recede symbolically at the end. Perhaps even the 'imprinting' steps of the final line continues with this conceit. All of the figurative images in the poem cleverly link to the poem's ideas of death, loss and family. The father is 'bound the living room with heat', a metaphor with restrictive physical, authoritarian connotations. The coat is personified as, again, an absence, 'waiting for a warm body'. The ambiguous image of the 'bare twigs edging into leaf' not only suggests spring and the passage of time, but might also imply that the family can live freer, less constricted lives now the father has died.

Making comparisons and planning a response

You should then be in a position to make connections with the specified set poem from the anthology, and plan and structure your essay. As you plan, you need to ensure that there are sustained, meaningful comparisons and analysis of methods.

Both poems respond to the loss of a parent with a complex ambivalence. The speaker in 'Effects' is trying to – belatedly – come to terms with his own shortcomings as a son and the distance between him and his mother. On the other hand, the speaker in 'Hollow' touches upon the possible dominance of the father, the restrictive weight of his absence and the tentative freedom his death brings for the family.

Listed below are some brief, potential comparative points on methods that could be developed into a response to this question.

- **Structure**: Jana's poem orbits around the father and his loss, but with a change in focus and a lighter tone at the end, as spring comes and the family head out for a walk. 'Effects' also 'orbits' in a way – it is constructed as a chain of different associations and memories as the speaker looks at his mother's hand. The end of 'Effects' is also a significant development. However, the tone does not lighten but darkens, with the incredibly poignant image of the 'little bag of her effects' confirming her death, and suggesting the distance in the speaker's relationship with the mother.

- **Form**: Jana adopts an irregular form, using short lines and enjambment to suggest the silence and gaps. However, Jenkins uses a largely regular form (many lines in rhyming iambic pentameter), the order of which is in tension with the overwhelming, uncontrollable flood of emotions the speaker is feeling.

- **Imagery**: The images of the dents in the sofa in 'Hollow' suggest figuratively the unique, irreplaceable qualities of the father and also the impact he has had on the family. However, the images of the mother's hands in 'Effects' embody her difficult life ('scarred', 'knuckles reddened') and poignant deterioration and death ('blotched and crinkled', 'fingers couldn't clasp').

Further practice

This section provides you with another opportunity to develop a response to an 'unseen' poem, using the process outlined in this chapter. Go through the different stages in the process and build towards a complete essay. A sample question is provided below the poem.

Begin by reading the poem carefully and with an open mind. **Establish a response** by jotting down some thoughts in response to the seven questions on page 64. Then read the poem again, in order to **establish an interpretation**. This will require you to identify the poem's (often implied) meanings or perspectives in relation to the focus in the question: what is the poem's attitude towards the shooting of the horse? What is suggested about the nature of violence and death? You will then need to read the poem again, and **develop a response** by paying close attention to the methods that Sheers is using. When you have completed this, you will be in a position to **make connections** with 'The Gun' and **plan your essay**.

Some of the sample responses in the **Working with the text** chapter also analyse this poem. You may find it useful to compare these responses with your own.

Old Horse, New Tricks

The vet was careful
to place the barrel of his gun
right on the swirl of hair
in the centre of her forehead.

In the silence after the explosion
she was still for a second,
as if she would stand in death
as she had stood in sleep.

We watched, an audience expecting tricks,
and eventually she obliged,
succumbing to the slow fold of her fall
with a buckling of the crooked back legs

and a comedy sideways lean that went too far.
There was little symmetry in her collapse,
just the natural pattern of pain.
Even her tongue was out of order,

escaping from the side of her jaw,
and dipping to taste the earth below,
like a child, stealing a taste of the cake
before it is served.

Owen Sheers

From *The Blue Book* (Seren, 2000)

Specimen question:

'Read the poem "Old Horse, New Tricks" by Owen Sheers and re-read "The Gun" by Vicki Feaver. Compare the methods both poets use to present violence.'

Taking it further ▶

The following poems all have meaningful points of comparison with 'Old Horse, New Tricks'. For each poem, identify some point(s) of comparison. You could then write and answer your own exam-style question, using the question above as a model.

▶ 'Giuseppe'
▶ 'Chainsaw Versus the Pampas Grass'
▶ 'The Deliverer'
▶ 'The Lammas Hireling'
▶ 'On Her Blindness'

Working with the text

Assessment objectives and skills

A01 Articulate informed, personal and creative responses to literary texts, using associated concepts and terminology, and coherent, accurate written expression.

▼ To do well with A01, you need to write fluently, structuring your essay carefully, guiding your reader clearly through your line of argument and using sophisticated vocabulary, including appropriate critical terminology. Use frequent embedded quotations to show detailed knowledge, and demonstrate familiarity with the whole poem. Your aim is to produce a well-written academic essay, employing appropriate discourse markers to create a sense of a shaped argument; it should use sophisticated terminology at times while remaining clear and cohesive.

A02 Analyse ways in which meanings are shaped in literary texts.

▼ Strong students do not just work on the level of vocabulary, but write well on the generic and structural elements of poetry. It is often useful to start by considering the larger elements of the poem's organisation, form and tone (and how they help to shape meanings) before considering the poet's use of language. To discuss language in detail, you need to quote from poems, analyse what you quote and use such analysis to illuminate your argument. Moreover, since, at times, you need to make points about generic and organisational features, being able to reference closely and effectively is just as important as mastering the art of the embedded quotation. Practise writing in analytical sentences, comprising a brief quotation or close reference, a definition or description of the feature you intend to analyse, an explanation of how this feature has been used and an evaluation of its effectiveness.

A04 Explore connections across literary texts.

▼ For both the AS and the A-level exams, you are required to compare two poems. You must try to find specific points of comparison rather than merely generalising. You will find it easier to make connections between texts if you try to balance them as you write. This will encourage you to consistently make point-for-point comparisons; you should certainly try to avoid writing about one poem and then the other. Think about the comparisons you are going to make when you plan your essay – do not make them up as you go along. Remember also that connections are not only about finding similarities; differences are just as interesting. Strong, comparative paragraphs could also begin with a similarity before exploring some subtle differences in attitude or method between the two poems. Above all, consider how the comparison illuminates each text, providing new insights into both poems. Some connections will be thematic, but make sure that an exploration of the methods used by the poet is at the centre of your response.

Summary

Overall, the hallmarks of a successful essay on *Poems of the Decade* that hits the three relevant AOs include:

▼ expression which is fluent, clear and accurate

▼ a clear, comparative introduction which orientates the reader and outlines your main argument

▼ a coherent, personal and considered argument which relates to the question title

▼ confident movement around the poems rather than a relentless line-by-line trawl

▼ apt and effective quotations or references adapted to make sense with the context of your own sentence

▼ a range of effective points about the poets' methods

▼ an awareness of the distinctive features of poetry

▼ sustained, meaningful and well-structured connections between the two poems

▼ a conclusion that consolidates your response and relates it back to the focus in the essay question.

Building skills 1: Structuring your writing

This 'Building skills' section focuses upon organising your written responses to convey your ideas as clearly and effectively as possible: the 'how' of your writing as opposed to the 'what'. More often than not, if your knowledge and understanding of the set poems in *Poems of the Decade* (and the unseen poem) is sound, a disappointing mark or grade is likely to be down to one of two common mistakes: misreading or not answering the question, or failing to organise and communicate your ideas economically and effectively. In an examination, you will be lucky if you can demonstrate 5 per cent of what you know; luckily, if it's the right 5 per cent, that's all you need to gain full marks.

Understanding your examination

It is important to prepare for the specific type of response with regard to *Poems of the Decade*.

If you are studying the text for AS, you will be invited to compare two poems from the anthology, one of which you will need to choose yourself. You will write one essay from a choice of two questions. You will need a clean, unannotated copy of *Poems of the Decade*, so you will be expected to quote relevantly, accurately and extensively.

For A-level, you will compare a poem from *Poems of the Decade* with an unseen, 21st-century poem. You will have one essay from a choice of two questions. The unseen poem will be the same for both questions. The unseen poem and the two specified poems from *Poems of the Decade* will be printed in the question paper.

Remember, too, that you must not claim any supporting material, existing criticism or reviews of the poems from *Poems of the Decade* as your own. If an examiner suspects that you may have memorised any unacknowledged material, they will refer your paper to the examining body for possible plagiarism.

Responding to examination questions

Step 1: Planning and beginning

The wording of the exam questions on *Poems of the Decade* is not likely to vary enormously. The main command is likely to be 'Compare the ways in which both poets…' (AS) or 'Compare the methods both poets use to…' (A-level).

You should identify the focus of the question (it often helps to underline it on the exam paper). The focus could be, for example, how the poets use interesting characters, or explore violence, or express anger, or present the loss of a parent. When you have identified the focus, you will need to make sure that your subsequent plan relates to this focus clearly and comprehensively.

A strong response will have a clear comparative argument in relation to the question, which is sustained throughout the essay. You should try to bear this in mind when you are planning and deciding which points to include or leave out.

Therefore, your introduction needs to logically demonstrate your understanding of the question. It will need to state clearly your comparative argument. You will only be able to do this well if you plan before you begin to write.

Student A

This student is answering the following AS examination task. Their chosen poem is 'On Her Blindness' by Adam Thorpe. This extract is the student's opening paragraph.

'Compare the ways in which poets explore truth and lies in "Giuseppe" by Roderick Ford and one other poem of your choice.'

In this essay, I am going to compare the ways in which poets explore truth and lies in 'Giuseppe' and 'On Her Blindness'. In 'Giuseppe', the villagers kill and eat a mermaid because they have no food. They try — and perhaps fail — to convince themselves that the mermaid is not a real human in order to justify killing her. They essentially tell themselves and each other lies. In 'On Her Blindness', the mother is blind but both she and her family do not seem to want to acknowledge this stark truth. Instead, they choose to ignore her illness or refuse to talk about it. For example, the mother would 'smile' when 'the kids would offer / the latest drawing'. In this essay, I will look at the form, structure and use of imagery in both poems.

> **Examiner's commentary**
>
> This student:
>
> ↘ has chosen an appropriate second poem sensibly, 'On Her Blindness', which explores truth and lies
>
> ↘ addresses the main focus in the question in a secure overview of the nature of the lies told in both poems
>
> ↘ shows a secure, accurate understanding of both poems, but has not developed a detailed interpretation of the poems' perspectives on the nature of truth and lies, and what they might be suggesting about human self-deceptive responses to suffering and guilt
>
> ↘ has not really adopted a comparative approach despite the fact that there is an overview of both poems. The student could have signposted the main similarities and differences in the poems' approaches towards the theme. There is no real sense of an emerging argument
>
> ↘ has used clear but straightforward writing style. Phrases such as 'In this essay I am going to…' are rather basic and lack the fluency required for a high mark for AO1.
>
> **If the rest of the essay continued with this level of performance, it is likely to achieve a notional low-grade C.**

Student B

This student is responding to the same AS exam question that Student A was working on, with the same choice of poem ('On Her Blindness'):

'Compare the ways in which poets explore truth and lies in "Giuseppe" by Roderick Ford and one other poem of your choice.'

'Giuseppe' and 'On Her Blindness' both explore the lies told to hide or deflect away from a difficult truth. Both poems therefore have suffering at their core. The mother in 'On Her Blindness' is shown to suffer due to her illness and struggles to 'bear it / like a Roman'; for her, it is a 'living hell'. Giuseppe (and, perhaps, the other villagers) suffers due to the guilt that he feels for his part in the murder of the mermaid — the poem concludes with Giuseppe unable to look his nephew in the eye. Both poems therefore explore the lies that people tell to avoid the suffering. The mother in 'On Her Blindness' keeps up the pretence that she can see, and Giuseppe and the other villagers try to convince themselves the mermaid is not human, and so can be eaten. Despite their widely significant subjects and varying forms—a deeply personal lyric poem and a magic realist fable—both poems have at their core an interest in how illusions are used to mask the reality of guilt and suffering.

A common method used in both poems to explore the brutal truth of this suffering is through a deliberately stripped down and rather stark diction. In 'Giuseppe' in particular the diction is unembellished, almost anti-lyrical:

> Then they put her head and her hands
> in a box for burial

There are no adjectives, there is no figurative imagery—just plain monosyllables. The brutality of the villagers' actions is allowed to speak for itself. The simple diction also lends the poem the qualities of a fable or fairy tale. Equally, the verb 'butchered' in the first stanza is not figurative hyperbole—it is literally signifying what the villagers are doing. The diction of the poem lays the truth bare. Similarly, the diction in 'On Her Blindness' is also literal and matter-of-fact:

> She turned to me, once,
> in a Paris restaurant, still not finding
>
> the food on the plate with her fork,
> or not so that it stayed on

This is a pared-down anecdote. Like 'Giuseppe', Thorpe uses simple words, and avoids figurative language and adjectives; his mother's 'living hell' is described directly. Elsewhere in the poem, Thorpe uses simple listing with similar effects. In poems about the challenges of looking directly at difficult things, a figurative, lyrical style would be less appropriate.

Examiner's commentary

This student:

▼ has a detailed and sophisticated understanding of the question's focus

▼ expresses a confident and original personal response to both poems

▼ keeps returning to the question's key concepts: truth and lies

▼ explores and evaluates some key methods required for AO2

- establishes a convincing, interpretive and rather compassionate argument on the way lies are used in a very human way to disguise suffering, guilt and doubt
- successfully continues and develops the argument established in the first paragraph into the second paragraph
- achieves cohesion and demonstrates high levels of organisation in the topic sentence in the second paragraph: 'A common method used in both poems to explore the brutal truth of this suffering is through…'
- establishes and develops sophisticated comparisons of both theme and method.

If the rest of the essay reached this level of performance, it is likely this student would be on course to achieve a notional grade A.

Step 2: Developing the argument and linking paragraphs

An essay is a very specific type of formal writing that requires an appropriate structure. In the main body of your writing, you need to thread your developing argument through each paragraph consistently and logically, referring back to the terms established by the question itself, rephrasing and reframing as you go. It can be challenging to sustain the flow of your essay and keep firmly on track. Planning helps enormously with this, as you prepare the sequence and development of your points beforehand. Here are some other techniques to help you:

- Ensure your essay doesn't disintegrate into a series of disconnected blocks by creating a neat and stable bridge between one paragraph and the next.
- Use discourse markers – linking words and phrases like 'on the other hand', 'however', 'although' and 'moreover' – to hold the individual paragraphs of your essay together, and signpost the connections between different sections of your overarching argument.
- Having set out an idea in Paragraph A, in Paragraph B you might need to then support it by providing more examples; if so, signal this to your reader with a phrase such as '**Moreover**, the idea that childhood is an age of joy and innocence is also suggested in the metaphors and similes…'.
- To change direction and challenge an idea begun in Paragraph A by acknowledging that it is open to interpretation, you could begin Paragraph B with something like '**On the other hand**, the idea that childhood is a time of joy is challenged by the shocking final stanza…'.
- Another typical paragraph-to-paragraph link is when you want to show that the original idea does not give the full picture. Here, you could modify your

original point with something like '**Although** it is possible to see the realistic elements in the poem, it could be argued that Duhig is also informed by the uncanny, supernatural elements of traditional folk music, specifically the border ballads'.

In your responses to *Poems of the Decade*, you will be comparing two poems. Your argument not only needs to be sustained, but also comparative. Your essay structure should balance the two poems equally with clear, signposted and sustained comparisons. Useful signposts include 'similarly', 'in contrast' and even the simple 'also' and 'both poems…'.

Step 3: Concluding: seal the deal

As you bring your writing to a close, you need to capture and clarify your response to the given view, and make a relatively swift and elegant exit. Keep your final paragraph short and sweet. Now is not the time to introduce any new points – but equally, don't just reword everything you have already just said either. Neat potential closers include:

- ◥ looping the last paragraph back to something you mentioned in your introduction to suggest that you have now said all there is to say on the subject: 'Both poems therefore refuse to condemn the lies, but instead express a compassionate understanding of how we need to maintain illusions and deception in order to cope with suffering and remorse…'

- ◥ reflecting on your key points in order to reach a balanced overview

- ◥ ending with a punchy quotation (probably from one of the two poems) that leaves the reader thinking, or which pithily summarises your argument in some way: 'So perhaps the poems argue that ultimately it is "up to us to believe" what is true and what is not'

- ◥ reversing expectations to end on an interesting alternative view: 'But maybe, with the inherent ambiguity and slippery qualities of poetry itself, the distinction between truth and lies cannot be sustained and the categories collapse in on themselves'

- ◥ stating why you think the main issue, aspect or theme under discussion is so central to the poems.

Student C

This student is concluding their response to the same AS exam question with the same choice of poem ('On Her Blindness'):

'Compare the ways in which poets explore truth and lies in "Giuseppe" by Roderick Ford and one other poem of your choice.'

Overall, I have demonstrated the similarities and differences between how Ford and Thorpe explore truth and lies in their poems. Using similarly stark diction and a direct, candid tone, they both explore the enormous gap between the truth and the lies which are told to hide or deflect away from a difficult truth. In 'On Her Blindness' the mother and her family are portrayed sympathetically as they prefer to maintain the illusion that the mother can see rather than face the difficult reality of her deterioration. However, 'Giuseppe' holds the community up for the nephew's and the reader's scrutiny and judgement as they struggle to convince themselves that the mermaid ought to be killed and eaten. As a fabulist, Ford's focus is therefore social, rather than personal; but both poems sympathetically chart their subjects' very human struggles to deal with difficult truths.

Examiner's commentary

This student:

▼ begins the conclusion with a rather awkward and unnecessary sentence

▼ includes a reference to the poems' 'stark diction' and 'candid tone', but there are missed opportunities to conclude with a comparison of the methods used

▼ maintains a clear comparative approach (AO4), with clear distinctions between the two poems made

▼ grapples thoughtfully with the key words of the questions

▼ has a flexible vocabulary, which includes some advanced phrasing such as 'both poems sympathetically chart their subjects' very human struggle to deal with difficult truths'

▼ shows a strong sense of a personal response and a secure, highly developed argument.

If the rest of the examination answer reached this level of performance, it would be on course to achieve a notional low-grade A.

Building skills 2: Analysing texts in detail

Having worked through Building skills 1 on structuring your writing, this section of the guide contains three more extracts from students' responses to *Poems of the Decade*. The next few pages will enable you to assess the extent to which these students have successfully demonstrated their writing skills and mastery of the assessment objectives, to provide you with an index by which to measure the progress of your own skills. All three extracts come with a commentary to help you identify what each student is doing well and/or what changes they would need to make to their writing in order to target a higher grade.

The main focus here is on the ways in which you can include clear and appropriate references to both poems; perceptive evaluations of how poetic methods help to shape meanings; and sustained, effective connections.

Student D

This student is in the middle of answering an A-level examination task which invites a comparison between 'Old Horse, New Tricks' by Owen Sheers and the set poem from *Poems of the Decade* 'The Gun' by Vicki Feaver. 'Old Horse, New Tricks' is printed in full on page 69 of this guide.

'Read the poem "Old Horse, New Tricks" by Owen Sheers and re-read "The Gun" by Vicki Feaver. Compare the methods both poets use to present violence.'

Both poems use form to shape meanings. 'The Gun' uses an irregular form, whereas 'Old Horse, New Tricks' uses a regular form. The length of stanzas vary in Feaver's poem, including a single line 'A gun brings a house alive' which emphasises the line's significance — the positive impact of the gun on the house and their relationship is confirmed. However, 'Old Horse, New Tricks' is written in regular four-line stanzas, which makes the poem flow and emphasises the story of the death of the horse.

The gun is the instrument of the violence committed in Feaver's poem. It is shown to have a very disruptive, powerful presence in the house. Its power to end life is announced in the simile on the fourth line of the poem: 'like something dead'. This is then developed throughout the rest of the second stanza as its stock is 'jutting over the edge', as though the table cannot contain the gun. The gun's violent impact is then confirmed as it is described as casting a 'grey shadow' over the 'green-checked cloth'. The contrast between the colour grey and the colour green emphasises the contrast between the death the gun brings and the life of the home. 'Old Horse, New Tricks' also uses imagery as part of its presentation of violence, especially towards the end as the horse collapses and dies. Sheers uses a simile in the final stanza:

> like a child, stealing a taste of the cake
> before it is served.

This compares the horse with a child. It is a sad but humorous image. It makes the horse seem innocent and playful, which makes her death more pitiful.

The diction of both poems is also interesting. Feaver in particular uses verbs to confirm the sensuous influence that the gun has on the speaker and her husband. Rather than presenting violence to be negative, the verbs suggest a more positive impact that violence can have. The verbs 'reek' and 'trample' suggest a sensuous excess. In the final stanza, the excess is taken to another level as the couple cook and eat the animals they have shot: 'jointing / and slicing, stirring and tasting'. These verbs confirm that the couple relish and enjoy the violence — they feel more alive. Just as the rabbits are shot 'clean through the head' in 'The Gun', the vet in 'Old Horse, New Tricks' places the barrel of his gun carefully on the forehead of the horse. However, Sheers' subsequent use of verbs contrasts with Feaver's: 'buckling', 'escaping', 'dipping' and 'stealing'. This pattern suggests the pathetic clumsiness of the horse's death as she performs her final, new trick. The verbs suggest the sad, undignified consequence of killing the horse.

Examiner's commentary

This student:

- ◥ has planned the response effectively, with three clear, separate paragraphs, each with its own focus (form, imagery and diction); there is therefore a clear focus on methods and patterns throughout the essay

- ◥ has benefited from the comparative structure, but many of the comparisons are straightforward and under-developed; for example, the comparison "Old Horse, New Tricks" also uses imagery as part of its presentation of violence…' is merely noting that both poems use imagery

- ◥ quotes frequently and always relevantly, although only occasionally are the quotations integrated into the student's sentence; this affects the overall fluency of the response

- ◥ explores Feaver's use of imagery securely and, at times, perceptively; there is an appreciation of how meanings are created. Elsewhere, however, the understanding of both poems (especially 'Old Horse, New Tricks') lacks development. For example, the analysis of the form of Sheers' poem — '[it] makes the poem flow and emphasises the story of the death of the horse' — is very straightforward and lacks precise detail. The student could have considered, for example, the impact of the short final line.

If the rest of the examination reached this level of performance, it is likely the student would be on course to achieve a notional grade C/B.

Student E

This student is answering the same A-level examination task that Student D was working on:

'Read the poem "Old Horse, New Tricks" by Owen Sheers and re-read "The Gun" by Vicki Feaver. Compare the methods both poets use to present violence.'

'Old Horse, New Tricks' is printed in full on page 69 of this guide.

Visually at least, the form of both poems is markedly different; the irregular form of 'The Gun' might suggest something about the disruption and excess of violence, whereas the apparently tight regular quatrains in 'Old Horse, New Tricks' suggests a degree of control, perhaps even a kind of careful framing of the horse's awkward death. The varying of stanza length in 'The Gun' is most clearly utilised in the fifth stanza, which is just a single line. This in many ways confirms and emphasises the turn that the poem has taken, away from an apprehension about the gun and its accompanying violence towards a recognition that violence and death make the speaker and the husband more thrillingly alive. It isn't just the stanzas which are irregular in 'The Gun': Feaver also crafts irregular line breaks to help shape the ideas in the poem. This can be seen in the opening couplet:

> Bringing a gun into a house
> changes it.

The first line holds in tension the contrast between the gun and the house. The line break suggests that the house has been disrupted in some way by the gun. The line break creates a pause before the reader's eye is drawn towards the verb 'changes' at the beginning of the line. This is a poem about change and the movement from fearful apprehension towards a primitive thrill. The lines throughout the poem are at odds with the syntax as the excess of violence develops. This can be seen in the fourth stanza:

> Your hands reek of gun oil
> And entrails. You trample
> Fur and feathers. There's a spring
> In your step...

The frequent enjambment and caesurae indicate a loss of control as the speaker and her husband succumb to the excessive primitive thrill of hunting. This is especially seen in the words 'trample' and 'spring' which literally run-on and overflow into the next line.

Sheers' form, on the other hand, suggests an attempt to exert a control over the violent event being described. Unlike 'The Gun', 'Old Horse, New Tricks' is comprised of five tidy quatrains, and the death of the horse is neatly and sequentially framed; we look on with discomfort at the horse's embarrassing death in the same way that the speaker (and others present) are an 'audience expecting tricks'. Rather than taking part in the violence like the speaker in 'The Gun', Sheers is here observing it in a more detached way. However, on closer reading, the quatrains are not quite fully regular. The first two quatrains describe the precise, medical way in which the vet shoots the horse. The lines are correspondingly short, and the two quatrains end with a full stop. As the horse's tragi-comic death is described, the lines become longer — perhaps because 'There was little symmetry in her collapse'. The horse's tongue tries to escape and so do the lines. The lines shorten again at the end, especially in the stark final line: 'before it is served', which emphasises how the horse's death came to an unnatural and premature end. So, like Feaver, Sheers manipulates line lengths but with very different effects — Feaver emphasises the joy in the killing, whereas Sheers uses it to build sympathy for the horse.

Examiner's commentary

This student:

- ▼ realises that the focus of the essay is on violence and refers to the poems' attitudes towards violence throughout
- ▼ writes convincingly about writers' methods — in this case, the particularly poetic craft of form and line-breaks
- ▼ forges very fruitful and interesting connections between the two poems' use of form and line; the first and last sentences of the extract frame the comparison effectively
- ▼ uses a flexible, critical vocabulary, with critical terms that help to achieve precision and concision as well as maintain a consistently analytical style
- ▼ embeds quotations seamlessly and ensures the writing is fluent throughout
- ▼ has a highly-developed critical understanding of the ideas and attitudes in both poems.

If the rest of the examination answer reached this level of performance, it is likely the student would be on course to achieve a notional grade A.

Student F

This student is answering an A-level examination task which invites a comparison between Alan Jenkins' 'Effects' from *Poems of the Decade* and an unseen poem, 'Hollow' by Rosalind Jana. 'Hollow' is printed in full on pages 62–63 of this guide.

'Read the poem "Hollow" by Rosalind Jana and re-read "Effects" by Alan Jenkins. Compare the methods both poets use to present the loss of a parent.'

Structurally, both poems resist a straightforward linear approach. 'Hollow' orbits around the father, his dent in the sofa and his corresponding loss, but with a change in focus and a lighter tone at the end, as spring comes and the family head out for a walk. If we accept that the father is presented ambiguously at best, with suggestions of a kind of restrictive authority, then the structure of the poem enacts the working out of the speaker's grief — she manages to break free from the orbit of her father. Therefore, the poem returns to the conceit of the dent in the sofa, the fact that they 'could not fill these cavities' — only he can. They sit in 'other places', at a distance from the 'shadows cast / by our father'. The mood lifts towards the end, perhaps as the speaker and the family come to terms with their father's passing. The imagery contributes to the lift in mood, with both spring ('bare twigs edging into leaf') and 'cool air spooled the house'. The trajectory is very much upward in the final stanza, as the family head into the hills, finally able to escape the shadow of grief and, perhaps, the authority of the father himself.

'Effects' also 'orbits' in a way — it is constructed as a chain of different associations and memories as the speaker looks at his mother's hand. He notices the scars, which leads to memories of his childhood and his mother 'scrubbing hard / at saucepan, frying pan, cup, plate'. He then notices the rings have been removed, which the speaker associates with her widowhood, and so on. This structure, alongside the poem's incredibly long, multi-claused sentences, contributes to the poem's sense of immediacy, of Jenkins (like the speaker in 'Hollow') being in the process of trying to make sense and come to terms with the death of his mother. Like 'Hollow', the end of 'Effects' is also a significant development. However, the tone does not lighten but darkens considerably, with the incredibly sad image of the 'little bag of her effects', which suggests how little the mother has been reduced to after a long life. However, Jenkins may well be

punning on the word 'effects'. Perhaps, even more movingly, he is forced to admit his shortcomings as a son (he 'learned contempt' and would 'disdain' her television shows) and how little effect she had on him as a mother. The two poems therefore use structure to convey the speakers' attempts to come to terms with the death of a parent.

Examiner's commentary

This student:

◥ maintains a tight focus on the question throughout

◥ has clearly planned effectively – the comparative structure is very well handled and there is a sustained analysis of the two poems' structures

◥ writes about writers' methods, but there could be more emphasis on the writers' craft

◥ makes some interesting connections between the two poems' structures and attitudes towards the loss of parent, especially in the consideration of Jana's lighter ending and Jenkins' poignant final line

◥ embeds quotations seamlessly and ensures the writing is fluent throughout

◥ has a highly-developed understanding of the ideas and attitudes in both poems and takes into critical account the inherent ambiguity of both poems (especially 'Hollow').

If the rest of the examination answer reached this level of performance, it is likely the student would be on course to achieve a notional grade A.

Glossary

Addressee: the person whom the speaker addresses in the poem.

Allegory: a narrative with two distinct levels of meaning. For example, Orwell's *Animal Farm* is, on one level, a story about animals who rebel against their farmer and set up their own system for running a farm; on a deeper level, it is about the Russian people rising up against their ruler and developing communism as the means of government.

Alliteration: the repetition of the same sounds, usually consonants, in any sequence of neighbouring words: 'judder like a juggernaut' (Agbabi).

Allusion: an indirect reference (usually to another text) that relies on the reader's prior knowledge. For example, the title of Adam Thorpe's poem is an allusion to John Donne's 'On His Blindness'.

Ambiguity: openness to different interpretations.

Anaphora: the same word or phrase is repeated in (and usually at the beginning of) successive lines of poetry (or clauses or sentences).

Assonance: the repetition of vowel sounds in nearby words.

Asyndetic list: a list which does not contain any conjunctions (such as 'or' or 'and'); for example, 'Cancel things, tidy things, pretend all's well, /Admit it's not.' (Fanthorpe).

Caesura: a definite break in the middle of a line of poetry, usually indicated by a full stop.

Colloquialism: the use of informal expressions appropriate to everyday speech rather than the formality of writing.

Conceit: a striking extended metaphor that compares two elements that at first seem very dissimilar.

Couplet: a pair of successive lines of poetry, traditionally (although not always) rhyming; any two-line stanza.

Diction: the choice of words used in a literary work.

Dramatic monologue: a kind of poem in which a single fictional character other than the poet speaks to a silent audience of one or more persons.

End-stopped lines: the opposite of enjambment; the end of a line of poetry coincides with the completion of a sentence.

Enjambment: the running over of the sense and sentence from one line of poetry to another, or from one stanza to another.

Figurative imagery: non-literal imagery, such as a metaphor, simile or personification.

Form: the overall shape of the poem, such as the length of stanzas and lines and use of rhyme schemes and rhythm.

Free verse: a kind of poetry that does not conform to any regular metre: the length of lines is irregular, as is its use of rhyme – if any. It may instead use more flexible rhythmic groupings and other types of repetition.

Fricative: a type of consonant made by the friction of breath, such as the f and th sounds.

Half-rhyme: an imperfect rhyme (also known as a near rhyme or a slant rhyme), normally in which the vowel sounds do not match, such as 'bills' and 'smalls' (Flynn).

Heteroglossia: the existence of varied and conflicting voices in a single literary text.

Hyperbole: extreme exaggeration to make a point or show emphasis.

Iamb: a unit of poetic metre comprised of an unstressed syllable followed by a stressed one. See **metre**.

Imagery: words that summon sensory perceptions. This could be in the form of visual images, but it could also involve the other senses – for example, the perception of a smell or a sound or a feeling. See **figurative imagery**.

Irony: a subtly humorous device in which words are given further – often opposite – meanings. For example, 'great' in O'Driscoll's 'into my great telephone bill' ('Please Hold') does not mean 'great'.

Lyric: a relatively short, non-narrative poem that expresses the mood or thoughts and feelings of the speaker.

Metaphor: a figurative device in which a thing, idea or action is referred to by a word or expression normally denoting another thing, idea or action. A common quality between the two is therefore implied. For example, 'I was his Jacuzzi' (Agbabi).

Metre: the way of measuring the rhythm of a poem. There are many different types of metre according to the sequence of unstressed and stressed syllables (which you might think of as light and heavy beats) used and the number of units of metre in the line. Iambic pentameter has five (pent means five in Greek) iambic units (a stressed syllable followed by an unstressed syllable). Iambic tetrameter consists of four iambs (tetra means four in Greek).

Minor sentence: A sentence which is incomplete. For example, Simon Armitage's single word sentence 'Overkill.' in 'Chainsaw Versus the Pampas Grass'.

Monosyllabic: having one syllable.

Octave: a stanza of eight lines.

Oxymoron: a figure of speech that combines two usually contradictory terms in a compressed word or phrase, such as 'bittersweet' or 'living death'.

Parallelism: the arrangements of groups of words or lines with similar word order. It can suggest a correspondence of meaning, or draw attention to a contrast. For example, 'My father's in my fingers, but my mother's in my palms' (Morrissey).

Patriarchy: literally means 'ruling father' and refers to a system whereby men have control over women; such power may be exerted directly or in more subtle ways.

Pentameter: see **metre**.

Persona: a fictional 'I' or mask assumed by a writer. See **dramatic monologue**.

Personification: the device by which inanimate things or abstract concepts are written about as though they are human.

Polysyllabic: a word consisting of more than two syllables.

Pun: a deliberate play on the different meanings of the same word, or words which sound alike but have different meanings. For example, 'prow'd on the cruisers' (Nagra).

Quatrain: a stanza of four lines.

Quintet: a stanza of five lines; also called a quintain.

Refrain: a repeated line, part of a line or group of lines. It can function a bit like a chorus in a song. It may have slight variations.

Rhythm: the pattern of stressed and unstressed syllables. See **metre**.

Satire: a type of humour in which the writer mocks someone or something, but with a moral purpose. This might, for example, involving revealing the follies of human nature, or ridiculing someone in power to undermine their position.

Sestet: a stanza of six lines.

Simile: an explicit comparison between two different things, actions, or feelings, as in Ford's line: 'But she screamed like a woman in terrible fear.' It can be more tentative than metaphor.

Speaker: the one who speaks the poem. It is wise to use this as the default term when discussing a poem. Keep 'narrator' for one telling an identifiable story and 'persona' for a speaker who is clearly not the poet.

Symbol: one thing (for example, an object) that stands for another, broader idea. For example, the dangerous staircase in 'An Easy Passage' could be a symbol of the challenges of adulthood. While a metaphor usually traces a correspondence between things and is often clear in its intention, symbolism works by suggestion or by calling on wider contexts and is often much more ambiguous – its meanings are more open.

Syndetic list: a list which contains one or more conjunctions. For example, 'cinema stubs, the throwaway / comment – on a Post-it – *or* a tiny stowaway / pressed flower' (Flynn, emphasis added).

Tercet: a stanza of three lines.

Tetrameter: see **metre**.

Taking it further

Books on poetry

Baldick, C. (2008) *The Oxford Dictionary of Literary Terms*, Oxford University Press
- ◥ An easy-to-use glossary, with entries on styles and movements as well as terms

Fry, S. (2005) *The Ode Less Travelled*, Arrow
- ◥ Engaging exploration of the poet's craft; especially useful if you are interested in writing poetry yourself

Ivory, H. and Szirtes, G. (2012) *In Their Own Words: Contemporary Poets on their Poetry*
- ◥ 56 contemporary poets – many of whom feature in the *Poems of the Decade* anthology – talk about their own poetry

Hollander, J. (2015) *Rhyme's Reason*, Yale University Press
- ◥ An enjoyable and wide-ranging survey of English poetry

Lennard, L. (2005) *The Poetry Handbook*, Oxford University Press
- ◥ Suitable for more advanced criticism, this book contains detailed discussions of all aspects of poetry

Matterson, S. and Jones, D. (2010) *Studying Poetry*, Bloomsbury
- ◥ An excellent guide to appreciating poetry that includes contextual and theoretical approaches in an accessible, integrated way

Maxwell, G. (2017) *On Poetry*, Oberon
- ◥ A collection of short essays on the nature and craft of poetry

Padel, R. (2004) *52 Ways of Looking at a Poem: Or How Reading Modern Poetry Can Change Your Life*, Vintage
- ◥ Engaging and highly accomplished critical appreciation of modern poetry

Roberts, P. (2000) *How Poetry Works*, Penguin
- ◥ A strong advocation of the importance and significance of poetry, with useful, accessible essays on poetic form followed by a wide-ranging anthology of poems.

Books of poetry

Sieghart, W. (ed.) (2016) *100 Prized Poems: 25 years of the Forward Books*, Forward Worldwide
- ◥ The Forward Arts Foundation also publishes annually its anthology *The Forward Book of Poetry*

Albery, N. (ed.) (1994) *Poem for the Day One*, Chatto & Windus

Albery, N. (ed.) (2003) *Poem for the Day Two*, Chatto & Windus

Astley, N. (ed.) (2002) *Staying Alive: Real Poems for Unreal Times*, Bloodaxe

Astley, N. (ed.) (2004) *Being Alive: The Sequel to Staying Alive*, Bloodaxe

Berry, E., Carson, A. and Collins, S. (2016) *Penguin Modern Poets 1: If I'm Scared We Can't Win*, Penguin

Byrne, J. and Pollard, C. (eds) (2009) *Voice Recognition: 21 Poets for the 21st Century*, Bloodaxe

Heaney, S. and Hughes, T. (eds) (2005) *The Rattle Bag*, Faber & Faber

McCarthy Woolf, K. (ed.) (2017) *Ten: Poets of the New Generation (The Complete Works)*, Bloodaxe

Padel, R. (2008) *The Poem and the Journey: 60 Poems for the Journey of Life*, Vintage

Websites

- **www.poetryarchive.org**: The Poetry Archive is the largest online collection of recording by poets reading their own work and features 14 of the set poets from *Poems of the Decade*; a useful resource for finding other works by the poets in the anthology
- **www.forwardartsfoundation.org**: The Forward website contains useful background information on modern poets and poems
- **www.literature.britishcouncil.org**: Contains excellent critical biographies of a number of the poets featured in *Poems of the Decade*
- **www.poetryfoundation.org**: A useful archive of poetry
- **www.rlf.org.uk/showcase-cat/podcasts/?rlf_front=1**: The Royal Literary Fund podcast series called *Writers Aloud* contains a number of interesting pieces on poetry. Julia Copus is a significant contributor
- **www.bbc.co.uk/programmes/b006qp7q**: *Poetry Please* is BBC Radio 4's weekly radio programme in which requested poems, including many from the 21st century, are read by actors and, sometimes, the poets themselves. Episodes are usually available on BBC iPlayer

A number of the poets from *Poems of the Decade* have their own interesting and informative websites and blogs. A selected sample:
- Simon Armitage: **www.simonarmitage.com**
- Ros Barber: **www.rosbarber.com**
- Julia Copus: **www.juliacopus.com**
- Tishani Doshi: **www.tishanidoshi.weebly.com**
- Roderick Ford: **www.roderickford.com**
- Daljit Nagra: **www.daljitnagra.com**
- Ciaran O'Driscoll: **www.ciaranodriscoll.com**
- Tim Turnbull: **www.timturnbull.co.uk**

The publisher would like to thank the following for permission to reproduce copyright material:

Photo credits

p.11 © philipbird123 - stock.adobe.com; **p.16** © MaryK - stock.adobe.com; **p.22** © Ian Sherriffs - stock.adobe.com; **p.27** © Upsidedowncake - stock.adobe.com; **p.30** Public Domain/https://commons.wikimedia.org/wiki/File:John_William_Waterhouse_-_Mermaid.JPG; **p.35 (left)** © Sergii Figurnyi - stock.adobe.com **(right)** public domain/https://commons.wikimedia.org/wiki/File:Jan_Vermeer_van_Delft_-_The_Glass_of_Wine_-_Google_Art_Project.jpg; **p.41** © Bernd Brueggemann/123RF.com.

Acknowledgements

Pp.9-10, p.58, pp.82-83: Patience Agbabi: from 'Eat me' from *Bloodshot Monochrome* (Cannongate Books, 2008); **pp.11-12, p.50, p.57, p.84:** The poem 'Chainsaw versus the Pampas Grass' by Simon Armitage, taken from 'The Universal Home Doctor' (Faber & Faber Ltd 2004) (ISBN 9780571217267); **p.12: Alexander Pope:** from 'The Rape of the Lock' (c.1712) public domain; **pp.13-14, p.52, p.58:** An extract from 'Material' by Ros Barber, Carcanet Press Limited, 2008; **pp.14-17:** The poem 'History' by John Burnside, taken from 'The Light Trap' by John Burnside published by Johnathan Cape. Reprinted by permission of The Random House Group Ltd. © 2002; **p.17: William Wordsworth:** from 'Lines Written a Few Miles above Tintern Abbey' (c. 1798) public domain; **pp.21-23:** The poem 'The Lammas Hireling' by Ian Duhig, taken from 'The Lammas Hireling (Bello)' (Picador; an imprint of Pan MacMillan On Demand edition, 1 Aug. 2013) (ISBN 9781447248200); **p.22** 'The Allansford Pursuit', a restored 17th-century witch chant (c. 17th century) public domain; **pp.25-26, p.82:** The poem 'A Minor Role' by UA Fanthorpe, taken from 'New and Collected Poems', Enitharmon Press, 2010; **pp.26-28, p.57, pp.76-79:** The poem 'The Gun' by Vicki Feaver, taken from 'The Book Of Blood' by Vicki Feaver published by Johnathan Cape. Reprinted by permission of The Random House Group Ltd. © 2006; **pp.28-29, p.52, p.58, p.83, 85:** The poem 'The Furthest Distances I've Travelled' by Leontia Flynn, taken from 'These Days' by Leontia Flynn published by Jonathan Cape. Reprinted by permission of The Random House Group Ltd. © 2004; **pp.29-32, pp.71-72:** The poem 'Giuseppe' by Roderick Ford taken from *Poems of the Decade: An Anthology of the Forward Books of Poetry* (Faber & Faber, 2015); **pp.32-34, p.58:** 'Out of the Bag' by Seamus Heaney, taken from 'Electric Light' (Faber & Faber Ltd); **pp.35-37, p.54, p.58, pp.80-81:** The poem 'Effects' by Alan Jenkins, taken from 'A Shorter Life' by Alan Jenkins published by Chatto & Windus. Reproduced by permission of The Random House Group Ltd. © 2005; **pp.37-38, p.52, p.84:** The poem 'Genetics' by Sinead Morrissey, taken from 'The State of the Prisons' by Sinead Morrissey, Carcanet Press Limited; **pp.39-41, p.53, p.84:** 'Look We Have Coming to Dover!' by Daljit Nagra, taken from 'Look We Have Coming to Dover!' by Daljit Nagra (Faber & Faber Ltd); **p.41: Matthew Arnold:** from 'Dover Beach' (c.1875) public domain; **pp.42-43, p.83:** The poem 'Please Hold' by Ciaran O'Driscoll, taken from 'Life Monitor' (Three Spires Press 2009) (ISBN 9781873548554); **pp.43-45, p.53, pp.70-72:** The poem 'On Her Blindness' by Adam Thorpe, taken from 'Birds With A Broken Wing' by Adam Thorpe published by Johnathan Cape. Reprinted by permission of The Random House Group Ltd. © 2007; **p.45: John Milton:** from 'On His Blindness' (c. 1673) public domain; **pp.45-47, p. 50, p.58:** The poem 'Ode on a Grayson Perry Urn' by Tim Turnbull, taken from 'Caligula on Ice and Other Poems' (Donut Press 2009) (ISBN 9780955360473); **p. 48: John Keats,** from '*Ode on a Grecian Urn*', (c. 1819) public domain; **pp.60-61, p.64-66, pp.80-81:** The poem 'Hollow' by Rosalind Jana, taken from 'Branch and Vein' (New River Press Limited, 2016) (ISBN 9780995480711); **p.67, 76-79: Owen Sheers:** from 'Old Horse, New Tricks' from *From The Blue Book* (Seren, 2000).